SHEPHERD
IN RESIDENCE

SHEPHERD IN RESIDENCE

by

Elizabeth
Creith

ScrivenerPress

Library and Archives Canada Cataloguing in Publication

Creith, Elizabeth
    Shepherd in Residence / by Elizabeth Creith.

ISBN 978-1-896350-49-3

    1. Creith, Elizabeth. 2. Women shepherds—Ontario—
Biography. I. Title.

SF375.32.C74A3 2012   636.30092   C2012-900540-1

Book design: Laurence Steven
Cover design and interior illustrations: Chantal Bennett
Photo of author: Courtney Clark

Published by Scrivener Press
465 Loach's Road,
Sudbury, Ontario, Canada, P3E 2R2
info@yourscrivenerpress.com
www.scrivenerpress.com

We acknowledge the financial support of the Ontario Arts Council,
the Canada Council for the Arts and the Government of Canada
through the Canada Book Fund for our publishing activities.

Acknowledgements

There are many people involved in this book, far more than just me, or even me and the sheep.

I have so many friends and supporters at CBC Sudbury that I can't begin to name them all. Ruth Reid recommended that I send samples of my work to Eric Moore, and Eric commissioned my first radio pieces. They kick-started my public storytelling career.

Nancy Pease and her husband David have been both friends and advisors for twenty years. I couldn't have asked for a better shepherding mentor than Nancy has been.

Bill Richardson encouraged me to write for publication. When he called to tell me he wanted me to write a monthly shepherding letter for his show, *Richardson's Roundup*, I think it's fair to say it changed my life.

Many people made a point of telling me that they listened to and enjoyed the "Shepherd in Residence" letters. Thank you all; the praise of an audience is invaluable.

Angie Gallop, Yvette Managan and Lucinda Kempe read the manuscript at various stages and made many suggestions. It's a stronger book for their help.

The Ontario Arts Council provided funding to help me complete the final draft of the manuscript.

Thanks to my publisher and editor, Laurence Steven, for his patience and humour with a fairly new author.

The sheep are all long gone to the sheepfold in the sky, but I'm grateful to every one of them. This absolutely wouldn't have happened without them.

Finally, and far from least, thank you to my husband, David Syme; thanks for fencing, for sharing lambing duty, for everything. I know it wasn't in your contract.

For David

TABLE OF CONTENTS

FOREWORD

ELIZABETH CREITH IS FEARLESS, inventive, seemingly inexhaustible, boundlessly creative, and deeply principled; she's the sort of person we all admire and, probably, would like to be. She also happens to be a very good writer, as I learned during my years shepherding correspondence for CBC Radio. Sometimes, she wrote for us on assignment and sometimes she wrote out of interest or concern for something she'd heard on the programme. Whatever the case, her letters—handwritten, by and large—were both thoughtful and entertaining: not an easy mix at which to arrive. I admired her humour and practicality and pointedness, and was impressed as all get-out—I still am—that she handled the rigors of rural life with such evident aplomb and still had the wherewithal to ponder and to wonder and to write.

All of these qualities are amply on display in the letters she wrote to the *Roundup* about the pleasures and the terrors of raising sheep. One of the privileges of hosting that program was that it allowed me and my colleagues the opportunity to create an office like "Shepherd in Residence" with the full knowledge that there was only one person qualified to do the job. Elizabeth Creith, of course, was that person and she did a bang-up job. Her letters were a wonderful addition to the program, admired and loved by listeners and presenters both. Sheep are eternal and hers is writing for the ages and here they are again, unwithered by age and in no way stale because of custom. I know you will enjoy them as much as I did, and do.

Bill Richardson. Vancouver. September 16, 2011.

INTRODUCTION

IT'S A GOOD THING I NEVER HAD a detailed map of where I wanted my life to go, because I'd have driven right over the edge of it long ago. Nothing in my upbringing in suburban Oakville, or my education in fine art and mediaeval studies, hinted that I would be where I am now.

The "where" is a seventy-some-year-old farmhouse in the hamlet of Wharncliffe. In the winter, it's home to about a hundred and fifty people living along a short stretch of Highway 129 and the Wharncliffe Road that runs off it. In the summer, there are more, perhaps double that number, as people come up to stay at camp. David, my husband, and I say we're in the 'burbs of Wharncliffe, because the sign for the community itself is a little farther up the highway than we are.

Wharncliffe is perhaps twenty minutes' drive north on Highway 129, the Chapleau Highway, from the Trans-Canada. The landscape is rocks and trees and water; blueberries, balsam, bears and bass all thrive in this country, and so do I. There are those who maintain that no matter what time of day you drive that highway, or in which direction, you're going to have the sun in your eyes. They say it as a matter of local pride, the same way Canadians brag about hard weather and mosquitoes large enough to carry off cows.

I'd say my life is an example, perhaps a cautionary tale, of how random interests and small events can drag you off that map. The casual discovery of a drop spindle led—by a road as winding as Highway 129—to life in the bush of Northern Ontario with sheep and spinning wheels.

Similarly, I think my career in radio can be traced back to a single letter I wrote back in the days when Bill Richardson worked on Vicki Gabereau's show. I'd heard a well-known doctor speak disparagingly about animals being easier to deal with than people. I wrote a rebuttal to his opinion, and Bill read it on air. Later, when Bill took over the afternoon slot with *Richardson's Roundup*, I was a regular contributor by mail and phone, often about events on my farm.

One afternoon I had a phone call from Bill.

"I want to offer you a regular gig on the *Roundup*," he said. "We'd like a monthly letter about what's happening with your sheep." So I became the *Roundup*'s "Shepherd in Residence". For just over a year I wrote about sheep and the joys and trials of keeping them. Although the gig, and the show, have gone galley-west, I look back on that time with fondness.

The sheep have gone galley-west, too. I miss them sometimes, and I'm grateful that I had them. I learned a lot from sheep. For one thing, I learned that the only way I could ever make them pay was to write about them.

And so I did.

WHAT'S A NICE GIRL LIKE ME...

SPINNING IS AN ADDICTION. Sometimes I think—especially when I think of my flock—that heroin would be cheaper. David, who did most of the fencing, believes that even if it weren't any cheaper, it would at least be less work.

I was raised in suburbia. I lived in Oakville from the time I was five until I was fifteen, and we never had sheep even when we lived in the country. My father and mother had a snowmobile dealership, and then rented construction equipment. Both had grown up on the farm, and neither was particularly interested in farming ever again. I've always loved animals, but it wasn't love of animals that brought me to keep sheep. It was mediaeval technology.

Ironically, it started in Toronto. In 1983 I moved into a house with some friends and found a drop spindle that someone had left behind. I recognized what it was, and bought a small book on spinning with a spindle in order to figure out how to use it.

If only there had been someone to warn me, some friendly recovered shepherd and spinner, to put a hand on my shoulder, look me in the eye and say, "Go home, little girl—this world will eat you up." Someone to take that drop spindle out of my hand before I tried it for the first time.

Here's how spinning goes. First you learn to spin with prepared roving, the gateway drug, all washed and combed and ready to spin. Then you buy carding combs and fleece to card into rolags. Usually the first fleece you buy is from a city store that caters to the dabblers in spinning. The fleece has been washed, and possibly dyed already. Many users never go farther than this. But for some, the hard stuff is what calls them. They succumb to the temptation to buy a fleece, a whole fleece, preferably freshly shorn from the sheep.

My addiction to fibre escalated—I needed a bigger hit to get the same thrill. I visited some friends in Ottawa who taught me how to spin on a wheel. While I was there, another friend sold me her first spinning wheel.

"I'm moving on to something faster," she said. Naïve little thing that I was, I couldn't imagine why.

Soon I was considering buying a set of carding combs and a washed fleece. I began to wonder how I could get a fleece straight off the sheep. Fortunately for me, sheep are in short supply in Toronto.

You can see where this is going, can't you? If it had been cigarettes, I would have started with someone's forgotten cigarette lit from curiosity and ended up with a tobacco plantation. If it had been alcohol, I would have begun with a sip of someone else's beer and ended up running a micro-brewery.

As it was, barely seven years after I picked up that drop spindle, I was living in the back of beyond with a spinner's flock of a relatively unknown breed of sheep. I currently own four spinning wheels, all much faster than that first wheel, which I sold long ago to another beginning spinner. I also own a loom and more knitting needles than I'd care to confess.

Among the livestock you can keep in the country, sheep are highly recommended by the homesteading types, because they are easy to handle and usually shorter than you are. They have a cuddly, endearing look to them, too, and a reputation for gentleness and docility dating right back to Biblical times. The lambs are cuter than anything delicious has a right to be. I think women who keep and breed animals also find some small satisfaction in the fact that female offspring are, for once, more desired than male offspring. It makes you feel positively warm and fuzzy just to think of keeping these sweet little creatures. At least, that's how it made me feel.

Along with all this, David and I wanted to be as self-sufficient as possible. Sheep are the ultimate self-sufficiency animal as far as I can tell. You can get meat, milk and hides from them, as well manure for the garden, and that luscious, soft, warm fleece. You can also get bruises, sleep deprivation, knee injuries, and a lovely little skin infection called "orf". In the rush of insanity that accompanied my entry to shepherdhood, I doubt if I would have listened if anyone had told me this.

I know that people have a romantic, dewy-eyed view of sheep and sheep-keeping. I still, at times, have it myself. But consider this a *caveat*, a dire warning, a cautionary tale about the potential life-changing consequences of curiosity. If I had tossed that drop spindle aside, today I might be the CEO of some Fortune 500 company, but no, I had to investigate.

Curiosity killed the cat, but all it did for me was land me in deep sheep.

Rabbiting on

I DIDN'T START WITH SHEEP—not right away. When I first became a spinner I lived within spitting distance of downtown Toronto. Sheep were not an option. I learned to spin with prepared rovings, wool that has been washed and combed into a fat, smooth, loose strand, ready for spinning. Later I spun with washed fleece that I bought from a supplier in the city. Although I could have bought raw fleece from someone at the Royal Winter Fair, my house mates put their feet down hard on the idea of bringing unwashed fleece, and the possibility of sheep poop, into the house.

The problem is, I'm a "from scratch" kind of person, and I wanted to get closer to the source.

When I went to work for my father in 1989, we moved out of Toronto and up to Elmvale. We had a little house, renovated from what had once been my dad's shop when he sold snowmobiles. We had lots of space around us, but that space consisted of maple bush and gravel yard. There was really no place at all to put sheep.

I joined the Huronia Spinners' Guild, and discovered that quite a few of the women in the guild raised fibre animals. Some kept sheep, but many of them kept angora rabbits.

Angora, the wool from these beautiful bunnies, is a soft, light, warm fibre that comes in a lot of colours and is delightful to spin, to knit and to wear. Best of all, the rabbits take much less space than sheep. I had space for a couple of rabbits.

My first two rabbits were Solomon and Sheba. Both of them were black angoras, which meant that their faces and feet were black, and their wool was a beautiful dark grey. They were gentle and easy to handle. I learned how to groom them, trim their claws and harvest their coats.

Unlike sheep, rabbits are usually not shorn. Instead, as the coat "ripens" and loosens, the rabbit keeper plucks tufts of loose wool from the rabbit's back and sides. A rabbit whose coat is ready for plucking looks fluffier than usual as loose hairs slide out and stick up beyond the rest of the coat.

Plucking doesn't hurt the rabbit—in fact, quite the opposite. Rabbits groom themselves vigorously, just as cats do, and swallow loose hair. Unlike cats, however, rabbits can't vomit a hairball. The good news is that the rabbit won't wake you up in the middle of the night with that distinctive "wuk-wuk-wuk-wuk, g-a-a-a-a-ack!" of a hairball upchuck. The bad news is that the hair packs up in the rabbit's stomach, a condition called "wool block", which, if untreated, can kill the rabbit.

Almost as soon as I got rabbits, I ran into the kind of weird ignorance that plagues anyone who keeps animals for a utilitarian purpose. There's always someone, thinking untarnished by any contact with facts, who is willing to sound off.

One woman stopped me in a mall in Barrie and pointed at my handspun, handknit angora hat, made by my own little hands from wool plucked from Solomon and Sheba.

"How can you wear that?" she demanded. "Don't you know they kill animals for fur?"

"News to me," I said, "but thanks for letting me know."

Solomon, alas, led a short life. I found him dead in his cage one morning. I asked the woman who'd sold him to me what might have happened, and what I could have done to prevent it. She gave me an answer that farmers everywhere know—sometimes things just happen. If you have livestock, you have dead stock. When we moved north to Wharncliffe, I took Sheba and also Neville, who was Solomon's half-brother.

I set up my rabbitry in the barn. With the help of a roll of one-inch-square hardware cloth and some J-clips—as well as a specialized tool to clamp said clips over the wire—David and I made some decent rabbit cages. We suspended them with wire from the ceiling of the barn so they'd be at a convenient height for me to feed and water the bunnies, and scrape out the poop.

Neville and Sheba, once installed, were the foundation of a rabbitry full of lovely bunnies in many different colours.

Oh, yes—colour. Gregor Mendel, the founder of our studies in genetics, almost started in the monastery rabbitry instead of the pea patch. If he had, they'd have called him "Brother Crazy Gregor", because the transmission of colour in rabbits is way more complicated than in peas, and we would probably still be in the dark about all things genetic.

This is because rabbits don't have one gene locus that controls colour—they have five, or at least five that we can track. They control whether the rabbit has a wild-coloured coat or not, whether the rabbit is black or brown, how the colour goes onto the coat, whether it's full strength or diluted (for example, black or grey) and, finally, whether the colour does something just plain odd.

I'll spare you all the grisly details—although rabbit people can talk about them for hours—and just give you a small example of how weird it can get.

At one time I had Disraeli, Lily and Jonquil. Disraeli had the classic black face and dark-grey fur. Lily was albino, and Jonquil was a beautiful orange rabbit, as orange as a marmalade cat, although without the stripes.

Genetically, however, all of them were black. Lily's genes had decreed that none of her colour would show. Under that albino exterior was a black rabbit who produced black bunnies. As for Jonquil, the "something odd" gene in him said, "Ya know, I think I'm going to change all this black colour to red, just for a laugh."

Well, really, I shouldn't have been surprised. The rabbit has a traditional reputation as a trickster, and if you don't believe me, think of Bugs Bunny. I once had a rabbit, Oinga Boinga, who mysteriously became pregnant by remote transmission, or maybe teleportation. Her cage was between the cages of two other female rabbits, and she hadn't been put with a male for a couple of months. All the same, apparently out of thin air, she produced a beautiful litter of bunnies. My only thought is that it had been a very humid summer.

Compared to that, whimsical colour changes are a piece of cake.

SHEEP-TO-SHAWL

THE IMAGE OF SHEEP AND SHEPHERDING is relaxed, peaceful, nurturing and gentle, but we have our exciting moments. Being butted by a ram, catching a reluctant ewe for shearing, the adrenalin surge of leaping out of the way of a flock of grain-mad sheep—all these spice up the calm, quiet, rural round of a shepherd's life. Nobody really expects a competitive streak in shepherds.

In fact, my introduction to sheep people came with the racing wheels, the looming deadline and the hard-fought team effort of speed and skill that is a sheep-to-shawl contest.

A sheep-to-shawl hasn't got the cachet of a hundred-yard dash, or the flash of a freestyle figure-skating routine with quadruple axels. All the same, at every sheep-to-shawl I've ever seen, or participated in, there's been no lack of interested, even fascinated, observers.

I saw my first sheep-to-shawl in November of 1989 at the Royal Winter Fair in Toronto. The terms of the contest are simple. A team consists of four or five spinners and a weaver. Each team brings spinning wheels, any other equipment (like a drum carder) they think they might need, and a loom with the warp threads already in place. At the beginning of the contest, each team gets a freshly shorn fleece. The team's mission is to spin that fleece into yarn and weave a shawl and wash it, all in four hours.

When I went to watch that first sheep-to-shawl competition I took my knitting with me in case I got bored. The wool never came out of my bag. I'd never seen so many spinning wheels in one place, and so many different ones. No two of the twenty spinners were using the same kind of wheel. I'd never watched anyone else weave on a loom before, and here were five weavers, all together.

I wandered from team to team, noticing that each team had one member in charge of carding the fleece and getting the carded fibre to the spinners, and that, as soon as each team member had half a bobbin of yarn, one of the spinners began collecting the bobbins and plying the single strands together in twos to make a two-ply yarn. Once the yarn was plied, someone wound it onto bobbins for the weaver, who paused in tossing the shuttle back and forth only to change an empty bobbin for a full one.

The competition started slowly, with only the spinners at work. One by one, as the first bobbins of two-ply yarn were completed, the weavers sat down and began the work of turning threads into fabric.

As one shawl after another grew on the looms, I saw that these weren't simple tabby shawls, alternating one thread up and one thread down. The weavers had threaded patterns into the warp, and now diagonal lines, diamonds, zig-zags and bull's-eyes marched up the shawls taking shape on the looms. The freshly-spun, unwashed weft threads, yellowish white with lanolin, contrasted with the washed white of the warp and made the patterns stand out clearly.

As the time ran out, the weavers worked faster. Forty-five minutes before the deadline, the first weaver cut her shawl from the loom and began combing and trimming the fringes. A few minutes later she was on the run to the women's washroom with the shawl, a bottle of dish soap and a hair dryer. The others followed in quick succession. The last weaver had only half an hour to wash and dry her shawl and get it back to the arena for judging.

I don't remember which shawl won the contest. I do remember that when they were auctioned off, the top price was something like a hundred and fifty dollars, for the skilled work of six women for four hours—not counting the time to warp the loom. It came to six dollars and twenty-five cents an hour; cashiers at the corner store earned more.

A year later I took part in my first sheep-to-shawl, again at the Royal, with the Huronia Spinners' Guild. We held a rehearsal to time ourselves and plan our strategy.

The rehearsal showed that we could easily get the shawl done in time, but the real bottleneck was washing it afterwards. Even with a hair dryer, it was impossible to get the shawl washed and completely dried in less than forty-five minutes to an hour.

It was our weaver, Annie, who had the brilliant idea.

"What if the person plying washed each skein of plied yarn before winding it on the bobbins? Then it could dry as the weaving was going on, and we wouldn't have to wash the whole shawl at the end."

"Could we get it dry enough to weave with?"

"Roll it in a towel and jump on it. That's what I do with socks," said Pat. "They're still damp, but not dripping."

"Can we take a microwave?" asked Jean. "We could microwave the skeins for a minute after the towel. That'll help the water evaporate. I've got a little one."

That's what we did. As each skein of two-ply yarn was finished, Jean washed it, squeezed out most of the water and stuck it in the microwave for a minute before winding the bobbins for Annie. Our shawl wove up soft and white, and we were able to get it completely dry by the end of the four hours. We came in first.

At the auction, our shawl sold for eighty dollars, a per-hour rate of $3.25 for each of us. This is why there will never be professional teams of sheep-to-shawlers.

First Fleece

After the sheep-to-shawl contest, I joined the Huronia Spinners' Guild. Every addict has her enablers, and mine were the ladies of the guild. About a quarter of them kept either rabbits or sheep, and most of them could speak very knowledgeably on the qualities of various sheep breeds and their wool. This was *terra incognita* to me. I was only beginning to come to terms with fleece. Wool was wool, wasn't it? Of course there were different colours of the stuff, like brown or grey, but, really, beyond that, what was the difference?

That began to change when I bought my first fleece. I went to Neil Meatherall for it. Neil came highly recommended to me by the ladies of the Huronia Spinners' Guild. He raised sheep primarily for meat, but he catered to the area's spinners by keeping meat sheep that also grew soft, medium-fine wool.

The Meatheralls took their sheep, and their shearing, seriously. It was a rare year that a Meatherall didn't win, place or show in the shearing competition.

One March day, about a year after we'd moved from Toronto to Elmvale, I called Neil and asked when would be a good time to come out to Glen Huron to buy a fleece from him.

"Come on Sunday about one o'clock," he said.

Sunday David and I drove out through the lovely, hilly country in which Glen Huron nestles. We found the Meatherall farm easily. As soon as we turned in the gate we saw the house, perched on a rise of land in the middle of rolling fields. The barn stood farther back to the left, surrounded by sheep nosing at scraps of hay.

Neil was just finished his lunch, and he got up and put his coveralls back on before leading us down, as we thought, to the basement of his house. It turned out that the ground floor level was open to the outside, high-ceilinged and concrete-floored. It was where Neil did his slaughtering. This was in the days when a sheep farmer could more easily meet the requirements for legal slaughtering, and Neil regularly killed lamb for Italian families.

"Did twenty-one lambs for the Italians this morning," he said. "Do you like white wine or red wine?"

"We like red," David said. Neil took a bottle from a tabletop crowded with different sizes of unlabelled bottles and handed it to him.

"The Italians always give me a bottle of wine when they get a lamb," he said. "I prefer the white. I cut it half and half with ginger ale. So how many fleeces do you want?"

"I want two," I said, "and I was hoping one of them could be black."

"Well, we'll see. Let's get some sheep onto the shearing floor. You don't choose the fleeces—I'll choose them for you. New spinners don't usually know how to choose a fleece, and I want you to have good ones."

The shearing floor was the second floor of the sheep barn. It was the work of a few minutes for Neil to move half-a-dozen sheep—including two black ones—up the long ramp from the ground to the shearing floor. Then he deftly penned them into a small space near his electric shears, which hung ready to hand from the roof beam. In a minute or so he had snagged a sheep, tipped her onto her rump and sheared her fleece off. He released the ewe, gathered up the fleece and laid it on a table nearby, then caught a second sheep.

There was nothing for us to do—Neil had this routine down so thoroughly that he could even make conversation while he sheared. I watched with mixed admiration and anxiety. I desperately wanted a black fleece; what if neither of the black ewes that Neil had driven up to the shearing floor had produced a fleece he would let me have?

When all six sheep had been shorn and released, Neil went to the table where he'd bundled the fresh fleeces. I went over, too, drawn by the creamy-white and inky-black fleeces, fluffy from shearing and shiny with lanolin. They were fragrant with that particular sweet, warm, pungent smell of sheep, a little like a wet sweater, a little like farmyard. Neil turned one of the fleeces shorn-side-down and handled it here and there, then picked up a lock, put it next to his ear and pulled on both ends. He did this with each fleece, and finally put aside one white and one black. I let out a breath I hadn't known I'd been holding.

"These two are good," he said, "I don't think they'll give you any trouble."

All the way home I could hardly wait to get my hands into that lovely raw wool. And Neil was right—both fleeces were beautifully loose, open and easy to spin, no trouble at all.

As for the wine, David said it best.

"If you dropped this," he said, "it would go 'plonk.' Perhaps we *should* cut it with ginger ale."

There's a postscript to my first fleece-buying experience. It came at the Royal Agricultural Winter Fair in Toronto, eighteen months after I bought that first fleece.

I'd gone to the Royal to take part in the sheep-to-shawl competition with the rest of the team the Huronia Spinners' Guild had fielded, and possibly to bid on some of the prize-winning fleeces.

After the sheep-to-shawl was finished the shawls had to be judged. They'd be auctioned with the fleeces later in the day, so I had time to wander over to the next little arena and catch the sheep-shearing finals.

It was no surprise to me to see that the four finalists were Neil, two of his grown sons and a man who'd worked for the Meatheralls. Each shearer had to catch and shear five ewes, also provided by Neil, and each shearer had a helper to remove the freshly shorn fleece and throw it onto a long table to one side of the arena. Don Meatherall had his brother Glen to help him, and as Glen tossed one particularly creamy and lustrous fleece onto the table I called out, "How much for that one?"

"Five bucks each," said Glen.

I have never joined a scrimmage for a Cabbage Patch doll or clubbed anyone for a Tickle Me Elmo, but I've survived a scuffle of fleece-maddened spinners wrestling for a chance at a freshly-shorn Meatherall fleece. I was quick off the mark, so I got in right next to the table, with my hand on the fleece that had inspired my question and—I'm told—a look in my eye that spelled death and dire destruction to anyone who tried to claim it from me.

A few minutes later, half the fleeces were in the hands of my fellow spinning addicts and the crowd had thinned a bit. Neil came over to the table, leading a young woman.

"Elizabeth, this is Carol," he said. Then he turned to her. "Elizabeth will see that you get a good fleece," he told her, and walked away.

I found Carol a good fleece, sound, clean and open. As I handed it to her I said, "You'll have no trouble with this one."

It was like a graduation.

First flock

One day in July of 1993 I suddenly discovered that I could catch goats. I couldn't run them down barefoot in some Alpine meadow, but in a ten-by-fifteen-foot pen, hampered by several feeders, I was able to get my hands on any goat in the pen that I wanted, and keep hold. As I had no previous experience catching goats, I was even more surprised than the goats were.

A rule of thumb I've tried to follow when adding new interests or responsibilities to my life is "one thing at a time". In 1989 I planted an herb garden. In 1990 I learned to pickle cucumbers and other vegetables. In 1991 I got my first angora rabbits. In 1992 I moved to Wharncliffe and started keeping chickens, ducks and geese, and in 1993 I acquired goats.

It's not quite as drastic a move as it sounds, because I got angora goats, not dairy goats. I wasn't prepared for a ten-month commitment to milking. Another bonus is that while dairy goats have spring-jointed legs, angora goats don't jump, and can be restrained by a four-foot fence. When a new friend offered me several three-to-five-year-old angora goats for a very good price, I took her offer.

There we were, with a tiny flock of three rather middle-aged angora goats named Nanette, Easter and Thistle. Although Nanette was nobody special in the flock she came from, she established herself as head head-butter among my three almost before we arrived at the farm. She was bolder than the other two, friendlier, more sociable, more pettable. More of a nuisance.

Before we picked up the goats, David built a divider in the barn to keep the chickens' feed safe from the new occupants. From sheep-keeping friends I knew the danger of sheep (or goats) getting into grain and bloating, sometimes even dying of overindulgence. David built a solid plywood wall, with a low door for the poultry to use.

"Too big," I said when I saw it. He made the door smaller. When we got the goats, guess who walked right through it? David screwed a piece of two-by four across it. Guess who ripped it off within twenty-four hours? When he put it back on with carriage bolts, it stayed. In the meantime, there were other entertainments.

In my naïveté, I believed that keeping the alfalfa pellets for my rabbits in a garbage can would prevent the goats from eating them. Nanette showed me differently. Goat farts powered by alfalfa are loud, and thick enough to be almost visible. I could happily have lived my whole life without knowing that.

Nanette also managed to intimidate our cats, even Neferu, who stalked the geese all over the barnyard. Neferu came within a foot or two of Nanette, gave her fifteen seconds of eye contact and decided that this was one hell of a strange goose, and too much for her. She beat a retreat that was just a shade too quick for nonchalance.

It took us a few weeks to settle the goats in. Then we were ready to take the next step. The same friends who sold us the ladies had an eight-year-old buck who was related to nearly everybody in their flock. They'd replaced him with a younger buck, and Hulk was going to be sausage, which is how we came to acquire him. We drove over to Iron Bridge to pick him up. There was no trick to catching Hulk. The rattle of a grain scoop brought him at a brisk trot.

An adult angora buck is impressive. Hulk probably weighed over one hundred and fifty pounds, and had a set of twisting horizontal horns over three feet wide. He was a bit twitchy because he could smell the females, who were just coming into heat, but couldn't reach them. I felt more than a little nervous of him.

We manhandled Hulk into our station wagon. Stuffed into a car, he looked bigger than ever. As we drove home, we became aware of another impressive characteristic of male goats.

The English have a lovely word for any strong, pungent smell. The word is "pong". It can be used as a noun—"That goat has quite a pong"—as a verb— "He sure pongs, doesn't he?"—and as an adjective — "Roll down the window, would you? It's getting very pongy in here". Our eyes were watering by the time we backed the car up to our own barnyard gate.

The pong of billy-goats is legendary, but in fact for most of the year, an angora buck smells no more goaty than a doe. In mating season, however, the buck feels an urge to make himself attractive to the ladies, to spruce up and get their attention. Nature provides him with a built-in cologne and applicator for this purpose, and for about two months he uses it lavishly.

To put it bluntly, he pees in his beard.

I once witnessed this little performance, and it takes much less flexibility than you might imagine. Of course, repeated applications are required to keep up the initial impact, and as the residue dries and becomes sticky, it acquires a layered patina of dust, chaff and, in our barn, rabbit hair. Hulk looked like a white goat with a black face.

My nervousness of Hulk was all unfounded. David promised to stay within earshot, in case this fierce animal took it into his head to butt me to the ground and trample me. We were careful never to turn our backs on him. It was all for nothing. On the third day we had him, the ferocious brute strolled over to me and rubbed his massive head up and down against the side of my leg, then stood with his eyes blissfully closed while I rubbed the spot between his horns.

I returned to the house that day, and for days thereafter, with my barn pants redolent of Hulk's peculiar cologne. I'd found out his guilty secret—he was a big, gentle sweetie. Once mating season was over, he wasn't even assertive enough to be the flock leader; Nanette henpecked him thoroughly. He didn't care. And there was something rather charming about him, content with his food and a little affection from his people for most of the year, until the time came again to be the beau of the barnyard and make his olfactory impression on the girls. It worked just great. They all got pregnant.

I was awfully glad I wasn't a goat.

***

As spring came on, and the girls got rounder and rounder, we began to prepare for our first crop of new kids. We were starting from scratch, and needed everything.

David made kidding pens out of two-by-fours and plywood, in panels that could be knocked down for easy storage. Nanette made it her mission in life to show him how easily they could be knocked down.

We bought veterinary supplies, both obstetric and neonatal. We laid out vast sums for baby bottles, injectable vitamins, plastic gloves, sterile lubricant, mineral oil, feeding tubes, and other stuff James Herriot never mentioned. Animal husbandry is the only pursuit which gives you licence to ask a man to whom you normally say nothing more intimate than "Two bags of layer mash, Marty," if he can order you a vaginal prolapse loop.

We carefully calculated the date from the first day we'd introduced Hulk to his harem. It wasn't very likely, we thought, that Hulk could have won the affections of all three of the ladies immediately. It was likely that the births could be spread over several weeks. Mostly goats can manage on their own, but sometimes they need help, so you have to keep an eye on them. That means checking the barn every three hours. David, who was working at home, did the three a.m. check, and I took the six a.m. one just before I left for work.

These things are futile, of course. The very second I opened the barn door on Monday morning, at 6:15, I heard a high-pitched bleat and rushed to the back of the barn to find Nanette standing by the hay rack with two tiny, still-soggy kidlets. The smug look on her face said, "Nyah, who needs you?".

That evening at six o'clock Easter had her babies, also twins. I wasn't home from work when that happened, or when Thistle had her twins at six the next night. Within thirty-six hours every goat had given birth, and I had missed it all.

Well, not quite all. Thistle had still not passed the afterbirth when I finally got home on Tuesday, and David was wondering if she had another kid in there. My hands are smaller than David's, so I was the one who got to pull on a plastic glove made for someone with an arm long enough for an orangutang, smear sterile jelly all over it and stick my hand into Thistle to feel around for little hoofs. There were no little hoofs. It was something of a relief; goats have only two teats, so every space at the milk bar was already full. A third kid would have had to be bottle-fed.

In a day and a half we nearly tripled the size of our flock. We were incredibly lucky, with the luck of rank beginners; three sets of twins, no deaths, no problems we couldn't handle, and, best of all, we'd only done barn checks for ten days. It could have gone on for weeks.

That last made us think. A normal goat pregnancy lasts one hundred and forty-five to one hundred and fifty-five days. All the girls had their kids in exactly the time that could be predicted had they succumbed to Hulk's charms on the first day he arrived.

The way we figure it now, he spent about a day and a half doing the job for which we hired him. On the strength of those thirty-six hours, he got three hundred and sixty three and a half days of free food, free housing, and free scratches on that hard-to-reach spot between his horns.

Some people just really know how to manage things.

OF SHEEP AND DOGS
AND DEAD GROUNDHOGS

RABBITS AND GOATS WERE FINE, but what I really wanted was sheep. My friend and shepherding mentor Nancy Pease made me a deal I couldn't refuse on four Romanov-Icelandic cross ewe lambs and one Romanov-Icelandic cross ram. We duly went down to Shelburne in our Chevrolet Caprice Classic station wagon to pick them up, accompanied by our five-month-old puppy, Keeper.

While we were visiting, Nancy and David's dogs took Keeper around and showed him whatever passes for a good time among farm dogs. They didn't stray off the property, and seemed content to have the youngster tagging along.

There was only one mishap; on the first afternoon Keeper made the acquaintance of the electric fence. The other dogs knew how to jump through without touching the wires, but Keeper caught a hind leg over the bottom one. When his paws touched the damp ground, we all heard the yelp.

Fortunately I was outside at the time, and standing where keeper could see me. When I called him, he came forward to me instead of backing into the field. I comforted him just a little, and in a few minutes he was off after the big dogs again. The only physical effect was a pink line across his thigh for a few days. The psychological scars ran deeper; but forever after he was wary of any strand of wire, electrified or not.

A couple of days later we were set to leave. We covered the back floor of the station wagon with straw and loaded up the sheep, who were all of eight weeks old and still only half-grown. Nancy provided a generous package of "sheep dogs"—sausages made from an elderly cow and an elderly sheep. We'd had some for supper the night before, and they were delicious.

As we tried to coax Keeper into the back seat, he rolled his eyes at the sheep.

"No way," he seemed to say, "not near those things. I'll just take the front. You can sit back there if you want." Fortunately there was enough room for all three of us in the front seat. David drove, and Keeper snoozed with his head on my lap, and all went well until about an hour into the trip.

That was when Keeper woke up and belched. This was not a polite little I-had-a-bit-too-much-kibble-for-breakfast burp. Oh, no, this was the belch of a pup who'd been introduced to the delights of ripe dead groundhog. From the smell, and the look on Keeper's face as he fetched up a second belch, it was no longer quite as delightful as it had been.

Belch, belch, and then—oh, no—Keeper heaved. His back curved up, his head went down, and the noise he made was "bluk".

"We need to pull over," I said to David.

"In a minute," he said, "I have a transport right behind me."

"No, we *really* need to pull over *now!*" I said.

"Bluk," said Keeper, his ears flat down, "*bluk.*"

"I can't," David said. "The sheep will break their legs—they're all standing up."

It must have been the word "up" that did it. With a final "*bluuuk,*" Keeper upchucked a generous portion of used ground-hog, almost entirely missing my skirt. The transport blew past us and David pulled over onto the shoulder.

With the help of a plastic bag and some of the water we'd brought along for Keeper we got the worst of the groundhog cleaned up. I got another skirt out of my suitcase and did a quick change, and we continued on our merry way. For the first few miles we left the windows rolled down.

Used groundhog has a pong more powerful than a buck goat.

THE KING OF BALLYLOUGH CASTLE

MY VERY FIRST EXPERIENCE WITH SHEEP happened in Ireland in March of 1985.

It was my first visit to Ireland, to Ballylough, the farm where my father was born and raised. The farm is about three miles from the village of Bushmills, whose claim to fame is a whiskey distillery dating back eight hundred years. My Uncle Richard, the third son in the family, ran the farm after my grandfather died. He kept cattle and sheep; my cousin John raised a few pigs and my grandmother kept chickens. There was probably also a vegetable garden, although when I was there it was early March, and still too wet to plant.

Uncle Richard was very interested in the wildlife and lore of the countryside. Later, when he retired from farming, he took up painting. He also began to compile a book of the customs and language of the area and of the time he grew up in.

He really seemed to love his own animals, too, not in the way that a city person might love a pet, but with a diligent and sometimes extraordinary care. There was talk about Uncle Richard around Bushmills. He'd had the veterinarian in to treat a dog, an unheard-of move among the farmers in the area, and perhaps considered all the more extravagant since, in spite of it, the dog had died.

When I was there Uncle Richard had a new sheepdog, a liver-coloured Border collie named Toby. Toby wasn't allowed in the house, nor were the Jack Russell terriers who lived in the barn and kept the mice down. Still, Uncle Richard was considered "soft" about his dogs. Having a veterinarian in for a farm dog was hard to live down.

Ballylough is on a quiet, paved road which leads, in one direction, into the village of Bushmills. The other direction it goes to Ballymoney, the nearest town with a train station.

A mile or two up the road in the Ballymoney direction is a gently crumbling tower, all alone in a small, fenced field that belongs to the Traills, the family who own the next farm. This is the last remnant of Ballylough Castle, and one morning at breakfast my grandmother announced her intention to take me to see it.

"Och," said Uncle Richard, "ye'd best watch out for Tex, then."

"Who's Tex?" I asked. Uncle Richard gave me a small one-sided smile.

"He's Traill's ram," he said. "He might no' be too happy to see ya."

"You mean he might try to butt me?"

"Oh-ah," said Uncle Richard "Oh-ah" was "yes".

"Well, I'll just get out of his way," I said.

"You do that, then," Uncle Richard said, but the sly smile he gave me made me think it might not be all that easy to do.

"D'ye mind that ram we had?" Grandma said to Richard.

"Oh-ah. Th'one that butted the Traill girl, then?"

"Aye, that one."

Richard looked at me, again with that half-smile.

"The Traill girls, they'd come for milk," he said to me, "an' we'd this ol' ram, y'see? An' one day he butted one of them as they walked home up the drive. Knocked her down, so he did, an' she dropped the milk. Then he waited 'til she was almost up again, an' he hit 'er again, so he did. Square on the backside."

I watched Uncle Richard drinking his tea and wondered if the problem with the Traill girls was that they'd been walking away from the ram, or if the ram had just been a particularly obnoxious one. I wasn't going to betray my nerves by asking if Tex was that aggressive.

Grandma and I walked up the road and through one field to the one that held the tower. As we crossed that first field, the ground squishing a little under our shoes, a small flock of sheep in the middle of the field stopped grazing and turned to look at us. They stood stock-still, watching, as we trudged closer and closer, and then suddenly turned all at once and bounded away across the field. They hadn't yet been sheared, and I think they must all have been pregnant as well. Their bodies—particularly their rumps—were round and fluffy. As they dashed away, those round, woolly rumps seemed to bounce in unison, and their undocked tails flipped with every bounce. I couldn't help laughing.

Then we came to the field of the tower. Tex's domain.

Although both my parents were raised on farms, I had very little experience with farm animals. Tex, lying peacefully under a tree at the far side of the field and chewing his cud, seemed huge to me, and Uncle Richard's warning seemed more serious now than his smile had made it. How big would Tex be when he stood up? He didn't have horns, but I was sure his skull would hurt a lot if he butted me. I wasn't anxious to take the risk.

"I can see the tower fine from here," I said to Grandma, but she, eighty years old and in a straight, tweed skirt and Oxford shoes, was already through the gate. If Tex charged, she'd be much less able to run than I was, and her nonchalance shamed me. I followed her towards the tower, picking my way through lichen-spotted grey stones half-hidden under old grass. If I had to run on this ground, I'd trip for sure. Tex turned his head to watch us, chewing, chewing, chewing.

I don't remember as much of the tower as I'd have liked, but I still have a very clear mental picture of Tex: his round, smooth head, ears sticking out to the side and flicking from time to time, jaw rhythmically rotating in a small half-circle and pausing now and again as he swallowed—and unswallowed—his cud. His fleece was creamy white, the ends of the wool bunched together in locks on his back and sides, and slicked down with mud closer to the ground. I kept a much closer eye on him than I did on the tower, and when my grandmother and I left the field, I walked almost sideways in order to continue watching Tex.

Of course the joke was on me. Tex might have been nailed to the ground for all he moved. I never saw any evidence that he even had legs, much less that he was an aggressive defender of his turf, ready to charge any foreign invader.

"How'd you get on with Tex?" Uncle Richard asked at lunch.

"Just fine," I said. "No trouble at all." And I gave Uncle Richard a little half-smile.

Signs of spring

Whether Wiarton Willie sees his shadow or not on Groundhog Day doesn't matter. Where I live, just east of Sault Ste Marie, six more weeks of winter from February 2nd *is* an early spring. We should be so lucky—significant quantities of snow on the ground in April is more likely.

When we kept sheep, one of our regular signs of spring was the resident ravens hopping around the barnyard, picking up stray bits of fleece to line their nest. When the loose bits were all gathered up, I'd see one or the other raven perched on a sheep's back, plucking out fleece. The sheep didn't seem to mind.

For any shepherd, the surest sign of spring is when the ewes begin to have their lambs. It's hard to believe, as I grew up in the 'burbs, but for me spring became inextricably linked to lambing. My dad grew up on a farm in Ireland, and I know they kept sheep. He never talked about the sheep, besides a passing mention of them, or about shepherding. He never told me about the amount of time you spend looking at sheep's butts.

You do this to see if they're "bagging up"—if the udder is filling out with milk. You look to see if they are starting to lamb, or

if they are passing the afterbirth, or if they are showing signs of inflammation after a rough lambing, or signs of mastitis. While they are lambing, you look to see if the lamb is coming head-first or in the breech position, or if it's stuck. Sometimes you have to get more intimate than that—pulling on the latex glove to reach in and disentangle lambs, turn a head, straighten folded legs or haul out a breech-birth lamb before it can inhale fluid and asphyxiate. And after lambing, you keep looking at the lambs' backsides to see if they have scours, a nasty, stinky diarrhoea that can stick their tails down and create all kinds of problems.

Now that I think about all this, I suppose it doesn't surprise me that my dad never reminisced about shepherding!

Our flock lambed early anyway, usually around the beginning of March,although one year we started on the ninth of February. That year there were a lot of black lambs cavorting in the snow. It seemed that our Romanov ram, Highway, had had a busy autumn. David swore that Highway had a smug little smirk on his face.

As soon as you have more than three lambs, they mob together and race across the barnyard, tearing around the adult sheep. They spring straight up into the air and bounce two or three times, a motion we call "sproinging", then charge off in another direction. They're delightfully funny in motion, and unbelievably cute no matter what they're doing. Those big eyes and small, delicate faces, the flipping ears and wagging tails, soft coats and tiny, pointed hooves make lambs look like just the most cuddly little animals on the planet—but catching them is an exercise in guile and agility. A week-old lamb can run like a hare, dodge like a ricocheting bullet and see out of the back of its head!

I was fond of all my sheep, but I had my favourites. Eystein, my black Icelandic ram, was a sweet old guy. I also had a little group of tame ewes—Michaela, Freyja, Folly, and her sister, Fudge. Later I had three younger brown ewes, Jynx, Kahlua and Kilim, but they never did become as tame as the older one.

People often asked me if I named my lambs. I named the ones I planned to keep, and didn't name anything I knew was destined to be eaten. By the time they reach a hundred pounds, lambs aren't cute anymore, and there are only so many rams a flock needs. The sad fact is that you have to sell lambs for meat because no shepherd earns enough from the wool even to pay the shearer, much less the cost of keeping a sheep for the year.

Lambing season was my favourite time of the shepherd's year, even though it was a lot of work, and a lot of looking at sheep's butts. While the roar of snowmobiles sounded in the valley, and the weather forecast still leaned heavily to snow and freezing rain, the lambs were a wonderful reminder that life was going on, and that spring would return. It made me feel warm all over, rather like a baby raven in a fleece-lined nest.

SHEEP LORE

I KNOW THAT PROSTITUTION IS OFTEN considered the oldest profession, and that some consider law the second oldest, but I say that shepherding has a longer history than either of those. Shepherding and sheep are rife with associations historical, religious and folkloric. Abel offered a lamb as a sacrifice to God, which He accepted, and Cain offered vegetable crops, which were rejected. I'm pretty sure that the acceptance or rejection of sacrifice had more to do with the offerer than the offering, but that incident may be the very beginning of the Judeo-Christian concept of sheep as quasi-sacred.

Some archaeologists speculate that sheep are the animal that humans first domesticated. They're smaller than wild cattle, and while adult sheep might be difficult to tame, the next generation of lambs would be easier. Lambs have an undifferentiated instinct to follow something large. "Lambnapping" a newborn from the mother and raising it to be used to humans might be one way to create a tame flock. Food is another. Whoever has the grain has a sheep's attention. When hikers in the Alps found the five-thousand-year-old corpse of a Neolithic man, one of the early speculations about his reasons for being there was that he was a shepherd out with his animals.

Originally sheep were probably kept as a source of meat and hides, later for milk and wool. They are more tractable than goats, and, some say, less intelligent. It's an interesting idea, especially in conjunction with the stereotype of sheep as good and goats as bad.

In addition to their meat, hides, milk and wool, sheep were an important animal for sacrifice and divination. Sheep, particularly lambs, have been considered a prime animal for sacrifice to the gods for millenia, to the extent that a sheep was an acceptable substitute for a human sacrifice. The goat was important, too, but in a different way. The "scapegoat" was a goat that was beaten and driven out into the desert to die, taking all the sins of the city with it. (We never say "scapesheep"!)

As for the divination aspect, well, in the *Aeneid* Virgil speaks of priestesses sleeping on sheepskins in order to have visions. Reading the marks on sheep shoulder blades is so widespread a form of divination that the list of countries where it isn't used is probably shorter than the list of those where it is.

It's lucky to meet a flock of sheep while you are on a journey. In England, a girl who wanted to find out whether she would marry or not could go out to the sheepfold at night and grab a sheep at random. If she grabbed a ram, she would marry, if a ewe, she would not. There is no record of what grabbing a wether ~ a castrated ram ~ would signify. A couple could predict the sex of a coming child if they cleaned a mutton (or lamb) shoulder blade of meat at one meal, then held the cleaned bone to the fire until the thin part of it charred. Next, they pushed their thumbs through the charred part of the bone to make a hole, and suspended the bone by the hole over the front door. The first person to walk through the door (except for family) would be the same sex as the coming baby. On a more practical note, quiet sheep predict quiet weather, agitated sheep predict storms and wind.

Lambing is a time fraught with sheep omens. If the first lamb you see has its head toward you, this is good luck for the rest of lambing. If it has its tail to you, this is bad luck. The first lambing is particularly significant—twin white lambs is a very good omen. A black lamb is a good omen if you follow the Kentish belief, but bad luck in Shropshire. As late as 1932, it was the custom in Shropshire to kill a firstborn black lamb to preserve the rest of the flock. In the Romney Marsh area a firstborn lamb should be rolled in the snow to keep disaster from the flock. Shepherds in England were, for centuries, buried with a tuft of wool in hand, to show St Peter that their frequent absence from church was due to caring for their sheep.

The Greek myth of the Golden Fleece was probably based on an old gold-gathering method. Alluvial gold (in rivers) can be "panned" out by letting the water run over a slightly rough or ridgy surface, such as a sheepskin laid fleece-up in the water. The gold dust collects in the fleece and can be shaken out later.

But I think my favourite piece of shepherding history and lore has to do with the Roman festival of Parilia, traditionally held in April. Shepherds decorated the sheepfold with green boughs and a wreath on the door and made bonfires of pine, olive, laurel and grass. Then they'd drive the sheep between two of these fires to purify and bless them. Wine was a feature of such festivals, and shepherds, when they had had enough wine, would leap over the fires to bring luck to the flocks and the pastures.

I'm all for re-establishing this festival in the agricultural community. Lambing in our flock went from February to mid-April, and I sure could have used a party about then. Maybe we should petition the government about sneaking another statutory holiday into the calendar.

SHEEP AT THE TABLE

NOVEMBER IS THE TIME OF YEAR that always makes me think of endings and beginnings. In the Celtic pre-Christian religion, the day we call Hallowe'en was called Samhain, and marked the beginning of winter. It was also the time when the veil between the worlds of the living and the dead, or of humans and supernatural creatures, was very thin and easily penetrated. The crossover from life to death, or from this world to the otherworld, and vice-versa, was easy to do. It was a dangerous time of year, charged with the energies of life and death.

In the fall, the shepherd takes the lambs to the butcher. The business of taking the lambs to the butcher is what elicits the greatest amount of negative comment from other people. "How can you eat a lamb?!" is one question I frequently got, usually asked in a tone of shock.

At first I would try to talk some sense to people—nobody cant afford to keep sheep unless they sell lamb for meat, because the price you get for wool doesn't even pay the shearer. Yes, they're awfully cute when they're born, but not so cute when they grow up.

Hay isn't cheap, either, although it's less expensive to buy it than to buy all the equipment you need to grow it. But it's strange how people who don't mind chowing down a steak or chicken have a mental block when it comes to lambs. Calves are pretty cute, too, and nothing elicits the "Awwww!" response like a box of fluffy, yellow, peeping day-old chicks. I'm afraid most shepherds get tired of this whole question after a few years. Eventually I gave up trying to educate people, and my answer to the "How-can-you-eat-a-lamb" question became, "Roasted with garlic and rosemary is good."

We didn't have lamb when I was growing up. I never ate lamb until I married my first husband. My dad told me that Mom had cooked lamb once during their marriage.

"I think she ate the leftovers," he said.

Later I coaxed the reason out of him. Dad grew up in Ireland during the Second World War. Although the local farmers were supposed to sell their meat to the government, most of them didn't do it, or didn't do it all the time.

"They'd give you tickets for meat at the butcher's," he said, "but there was never anything good there. We used to just kill our own on the farm and dress it out."

"Didn't anyone report you?" I asked.

He shrugged.

"Everyone did it," he said, "and anyway, the constable sat halfway up the driveway on his motorcycle, keeping watch in case anyone came along. He always went home with a little package under his arm."

"So why don't you like lamb? I mean, you were used to eating it, right?"

"We never got lamb," he said, "it was always mutton, the old sheep. I never wanted to taste a sheep again after that."

If you're keeping a flock of constant size, shepherding practice says that you should replace twenty percent of your ewes each year. That means taking some of your old ewes to the butcher as well.

The older ewes' meat is not generally salable, certainly not as lamb, and there is a widespread opinion in North America that older sheep, mutton, tastes far too strong. When Fafnir, one of my rams, wore out his welcome and went for the little tour of Northern Quality meats, my sister-in-law Jennifer requested a whole leg of Fafnir. Jennifer is a creative and adventuresome cook; the leg of ram was for a recipe she wanted to try.

The recipe involved marinating the leg in red wine and a bunch of other stuff, then cooking it. The marinating process took nearly a week, as I recall, and the end product was very strong-tasting. Although I have had game several times, this was the first meal I've ever eaten to which the word "gamy" actually applied. The family's opinion was that it was fine, but not a meal you'd want to eat *every* year.

Fafnir, however, was four years old when he hit the table. My friend Nancy Pease very sensibly turns these older animals into sausage, usually mixed with beef from a similarly elderly animal from her husband David's herd of Salers cattle. She calls the resulting sausages by the witty name of "sheepdogs", and very good they are, too. We used most of our older ewes ourselves for meatballs and stew. I once culled an eighteen-month-old ram actually during breeding season, when you would expect the taste to be pretty—well, rammy. He tasted a little stronger than lamb, but not a lot. Quite pleasant, really. On the other hand, one of my customers has specifically requested a couple of older sheep this year, as her father complained last year that the lamb had no flavour. *Chacun à son gout* definitely applies here.

The year is a circle, as the ancient Celts knew, and the end and the beginning are separated by the thinnest of partitions. While I loaded up the lambs for the trip to the butcher, the rams and ewes were doing that oldest dance, getting my next crop of lambs started and setting up a whole lot of work for me a few months down the road.

Boys and girls together

ALTHOUGH LAMBING SEEMS LIKE THE BEGINNING of the shepherd's year, autumn is really where life begins and ends for the sheep. Autumn was when I chose the lambs that I planned to keep and sent the rest, as well as some of the ewes, off to the butcher.

Meanwhile, in the barnyard, Laughing Boy and Highway butted heads, grunting and chasing each other and bumping around in an attempt to monopolize the turf, and the attentions of the ladies. In between the rounds of this testosterone match, they followed the ewes. There is no mistaking this for a casual "Oh, is there some good grazing up there, mind if I join you?" *That* is usually conducted at a sedate amble, whereas the courtship chase is usually at a fast walk, bordering on a trot. The ram has his neck stretched out and his nose as close as the ewe will let him get to, let us say, the centre of interest. Rams don't use pickup lines—they cut straight to "Hey, baby, do ya wanna?"

There is also something refreshingly direct about the response of the ewes. If she does wanna, there are no further negotiations. Once, when I had a teenage girl visiting the farm, she saw the sheep *in flagrante delicto*. Crimson-faced, she asked me "Don't they even wait for it to get dark?" I told her that animals didn't care about that, and she turned even redder.

If the ewe doesn't wanna, she also has a direct response. She squats and urinates on the ground in front of the ram. Talk about being told to piss off! Of course, a direct response is needed—the rams are pretty single-minded about the whole thing, and within a minute or two of being rebuffed, they'll be back for more.

Traditionally, when a shepherd wants to breed efficiently, the ewes and rams are kept in separate pastures, and introduced only at breeding time. Someone who wants to conserve the ram's energy can accurately pick out ewes that are in season by introducing what is called a "teaser ram" into the ewe flock. This is a ram who is either vasectomized, or, more commonly, dressed in a leather apron that prevents him from taking advantage of the situation with a willing ewe. He pinpoints the ewes who are in season, and they are removed from the flock and taken to the ram who gets to do the breeding. I've often wondered why this aproned ram is called a "teaser ram". It seems to me he ought to be called a "teased ram".

Once all the ewes have been "settled", the big job for which the ram is hired is over for the year. Barring a predator getting through the fence—admittedly more of a hazard when you are as close to the bush as we are—all the rams have to do for the rest of the year is eat and sleep. Now and again I've had a male visitor remark that he'd like that sort of job. I doubt if it would keep its appeal for long. Shepherds are well advised to keep one ram for every twenty-five ewes, as the business of getting all those ewes settled in a three-to-six-week period is wearing, and a ram with a large flock to serve can get pretty ragged.

There's a joke among shepherds. "You know why sheep have four hooves, don't you? It's to remind them of the four most important things in life—food, food, sex and food." Although I've never noticed that any of my rams neglect to eat during breeding season, I think the four hooves switch from "food, food, sex and food" to "sex, sex, food and sex" for these few weeks. The ewes have pretty much the same attitude when they're willing. On one occasion the rams broke out of their pasture and I watched Elsie accept the attention of four rams in quick succession. She had triplets that year—David and I joked that one ram must have been shooting blanks.

We could tell when all the girls were pregnant by the way the rams completely lost interest in them, and vice-versa. If we were lucky, every one of our ewes had been bred by the end of the first seventeen-day heat cycle. If not, and breeding went on for another seventeen days, lambing could drag on for six weeks. We never again had the beginners' luck of a thirty-six-hour lambing season, as we'd had with Hulk and his harem.

Shortly after breeding season ended, the pasture died off for the winter. We drained the water line to the barn with the first hard frost, and began the routine of carrying buckets and hauling hay. Aside from the twice-a-day muscling of feed and water out to the barn, winter was a peaceful time. There was no fencing to be done, no barn checks, just the anticipation of spring as I watched my ewes gradually grow round and fat with their lambs.

WOMAN'S BEST FRIEND

WHERE YOU HAVE SHEEP, you almost always have sheepdogs.

In New Zealand, where sheep outnumber people by fifty-to-one, dogs are an essential part of shepherding. One well-trained and obsessive border collie can do more than ten men to round up a flock of mountain-grazing sheep and bring them safely home.

I'm a dog person, and I like herding dogs. They're smart and attentive and have been bred to look to people for direction. I also like mutts, particularly those with some herding dog in their background.

The dogs I grew up with were strictly pets, with no work to do. The dogs I kept during my shepherding years were working dogs, as well as pets. We had four dogs during the time we had sheep; Keeper, Brandy, Oscar and Garm.

As they learned their jobs, I learned, too. If they didn't always do what I wanted, I began to understand that it wasn't stubbornness, or stupidity, but simply miscommunication. They wanted to please me—they just didn't always understand how to do it. Over time I learned how they thought, and how to work with them to provide clear signals. When we were at our best, I felt like the dog and I were a team.

Even so, just as I learned that sheep don't think like humans, I learned that dogs don't, either, no matter how much we may want to anthropomorphize them.

Keeper was border collie and German shepherd, with some other unspecified stuff swimming around in his gene pool. After his initial fear of the lambs we brought home in the back of the station wagon, he developed into a good, reliable dog around the sheep.

Keeper initially believed that sheep should be in the barn at all times, and made it his business to put them back whenever he caught them outside. Eventually I got him trained to let them out to graze, and then to help me move them where I wanted them. We didn't use the conventional signals - "away to me", "come by" and the like. Instead I would direct Keeper to stand somewhere, effectively blocking the sheep from bolting in his direction. On my command, he would walk slowly towards me and help me edge the sheep where I wanted them to go. It worked pretty well.

Later we got Brandy. Brandy was a pretty brown mongrel who might have been smart if he hadn't decided, shortly after we got him, to join the rams in their head-butting contests. He got caught between Fafnir and Barley, and we believe the impact cracked his skull. He developed a massive abscess on his head, which had to be drained, and ever after he was a happy idiot. In a specialized way he was clever. He could, and did, walk on logs and branches, and once on the outside rim of the truck cap. He seemed to enjoy it, and his footing was sure. It took him months, however, to learn the simplest commands.

Keeper was David's favourite dog, but Garm was mine. Garm, like our other dogs, was a farm puppy. His mother was half German shepherd, and we suspected that his father might have been a Newfoundland cross. He was a big black dog, gentle where Keeper was assertive, tolerant of children, lambs and cats to a remarkable degree.

Shortly after we got Garm, David went to work full-time in Sault Ste Marie, and Garm was at home with me and the sheep. He accompanied me to the barn on lambing checks and hay runs. During lambing, when I wanted to look at the ewes without disturbing them, I could ask Garm to wait partway up the path to the barn and know that he would sit or lie there quietly until I came back. Like Keeper, he learned quickly to sit or stand where I put him and to walk up slowly towards me to move the sheep.

Why, with sheep, did I not have a border collie? One consideration was money. At the time, a border collie puppy was six hundred dollars. A trained dog was much more. Border collies are good workers—too good. Many of them are workaholics, too driven and obsessive about herding to make good companions. They're extremely energetic, and often over-enthusiastic about their work.

I didn't have the money for a puppy, let alone a trained dog, and I didn't have the know-how to train a border collie myself. Besides, I didn't know how I'd keep a dog of that energy level occupied and worn out enough to leave me a quiet evening. Keeper and Garm learned enough for the purpose, and I could work with them. They were also content to lie on the living room floor in the evening, as long as they could be with us. Brandy, too, was happy to be a couch potato.

The only dog I failed was Oscar. He was fourteen months old when I got him, a few months after Brandy argued with a car and came off second best. Oscar had already had three homes, plus the pound. I don't know what I was thinking, except that he was a sweet dog who needed a lot of discipline and a lot of love.

The love wasn't the hard part. In spite of his sad history, he was a trusting and affectionate dog. He got along immediately with Garm, although it took him a week or so to learn not to chase the cats.

But his heredity, as well as his history, told against him. He was half husky, half border collie, and he loved to chase. Cars, cats, anything that looked like it was running away, he was on it. I tried to break him of it. Except for limited success with the cats, and keeping him from chasing my own sheep, I couldn't do it. Worse still, Garm began to run with him.

Eventually he discovered the neighbour's sheep. One June night, about a year after I got him, he caught a lamb and tore its leg. The neighbour called me, and I went to collect Oscar and assess the damage.

"I caught him in the pen," she said, when I'd put Oscar in the car. I knew she'd got him dead to rights. The only reason he left my sheep alone is that I'd done some very hard training, and I kept an eye on him.

A long, narrow strip of skin dangled from the lamb's hind leg, but it was already eating again. The damage was minimal, and I'd seen sheep hurt worse and still recover. All the same, I knew what had to be done. It would be completely irresponsible to pass him on to another owner, and a life at the end of a chain is no life for a dog.

I didn't have a gun, but my neighbour Les came over with his. I put Oscar on a leash, for the first time since I'd brought him home. I told him to sit, and told him he was a good boy. He gave me the sweet look he always had when I praised him. And then Les shot him, and he keeled over, dead before he hit the ground.

I cried, not only for his death, but for the poor handling that had spoiled him before I got him, and my own inability to rehabilitate him.

When David came home, we buried Oscar at the edge of the bush, past the barn. I found a large piece of granite, rounded on one side, flat on the other, and placed it at the head of the mound. Garm sat by, looking confused and unhappy. When we finished, he sniffed over the mounded earth.

"He was such a sweet dog," I said through my tears, "and I couldn't help him."

"You did everything you could," David said, "Maybe nobody could have helped him."

He carried the shovel in his right hand and held me, still crying, in the curve of his left arm as we walked away. Halfway down to the house he looked back to call Garm, and began to laugh.

Wiping my eyes, I turned to see what could possibly be funny.

Garm was crouched on Oscar's grave, producing an enormous pile of crap. I couldn't help it; even though I was still crying, I started to laugh, too. The combination nearly choked me. David was bent double, gasping for breath.

When we could talk again we agreed that Garm had been marking an important place in the only way he knew, a doggy "in memoriam" for his late companion.

CROSS-COUNTRY SHEEP

SHEEP ARE ESCAPE ARTISTS. We've herded sheep from out of our front yard, from across the highway, from two kilometres away in the Wharncliffe Cemetery and even farther from home than that, off the Wells and Rayner hydroelectric dams.

In the first year that I kept sheep, we'd hardly had to herd them from any farther away than the end of the driveway. One morning a woman called.

"Hi, I'm Sherry, Todd's girlfriend. One of your sheep is down here at Todd's place."

Ouch! Todd was an officer in the Ontario Provincial Police. I certainly didn't want any trouble with him.

"We'll be right down!" I told her, and hung up before she had a chance to say good-bye.

The first thing I did was run out to the barnyard and look at my sheep to see who we were dealing with. The answer was, "nobody we knew". The ewes Claudia, No-Name, Specs and Elsie, and Odd, the ram, were all grazing peacefully in front of the barn. I went up to the woodworking shop over the barn, where David was doing something woodshoppy with the table saw.

"There's a sheep down at Todd's," I told him when the whine of the table saw died down. "I think we should go see about it. It's not one of ours, but she thinks it is."

David shrugged and came out to the car with me. We loaded Keeper into the back of the station wagon and drove the half-kilometre down the valley to Todd's place.

When we got there, we saw Sherry standing on the front deck watching for us. Sherry is a short, slim woman, and she was clearly nervous of the sheep grazing under the apple tree in the front yard.

He—and he was quite obviously "he"—was a big, white, rectangular sheep with legs like tree-trunks and a round skull that looked like it could do some serious damage. He lifted his head to look around at us as we drove in. I saw Sherry jump when he moved and edge a little farther along the deck, hanging on to the rail.

David and I got out, and Keeper jumped over the back seat and came to stand beside me.

The ram turned and looked at us. We started walking towards him, Keeper at our heels, and he shook himself and ambled towards us with an air of, "Oh, look. Sheep people!" I put a hand under his chin and one behind his head, and he came docilely along to the car. David and Keeper followed in case he tried to break away, but he acted as if he'd only been waiting for us to turn up and give him a ride. At the car, he stood calmly while David put down the tailgate, and hopped into the back of the station wagon like he'd been doing it all his life.

"Is he yours?" Sherry called from the deck.

"Not ours," David said, "I don't know where he came from."

"Maybe the bear chased him here," Sherry said. "There was a bear cub in the apple tree when I got here this morning."

"And you just walked by it?" I asked.

She shrugged. "Yeah, I guess."

On the way back up the hill to our own driveway I pondered how a woman who would fearlessly walk past a bear cub in a tree could be afraid of a sheep.

We didn't want to put the ram in with our ewes. We didn't know where he'd come from so we considered him under quarantine. When we got home, we put Keeper's collar on the ram, drove a rotating dog stake into the ground near the garage and tethered him to it. As we got him out of the car, the girls lined up at the fence, craning their necks.

"Look, a new man!" they seemed to be saying. For his part, the ram trotted as far as the light dog-chain would allow and then leaned against the collar and curled his lip back, exposed his upper gums (sheep don't have upper incisors) and inhaled. This is called "flehmen", and it's the sheepy equivalent of "Ooh-la-la!"

By the time I got back into the house, the phone was ringing again.

"Hello?"

"Hi, I'm Bonnie Gareau. I think you have my sheep!" The Gareaus lived a good fifteen kilometres away by road, probably eight or nine cross-country for a sheep.

In fifteen minutes Bonnie and her husband, Lee, arrived with their stake truck to take charge of their runaway. He'd been missing since early that morning.

"I got him as company for the horse," Bonnie explained, "and when I went out to feed them this morning, he was gone. I think Gypsy opened the gate for him. She can do that."

"What would bring him all this way?" Lee mused as he closed the tailgate of the truck.

The ram's craned neck over the back of the truck, his flared nostrils as he watched the girls crowded up against the fence, told David and me exactly what.

SHEEP IN WINTER

THE WORK OF KEEPING SHEEP through the winter revolved around food and water. Worming, flushing, breeding and butchering were all past—lambing, shearing, and vaccinations several months away. Responsibility scaled down to seeing that the hay went out twice a day and that the critters had water to drink.

Fence repair, to David's relief, was also on hold for the winter. At this point, all our fences could fall flat on the ground and the sheep would go nowhere. Why bother? If they just hung around the barn, the sheep version of Meals on Wheels turned up on schedule. Once the snow had come and gone, David once again made the rounds to deal with the ravages of snow, fallen trees, rampaging moose and so on before we turned the flock out to pasture.

A harsh winter could make every trip to the barn a little arctic trek. No matter how well I wrapped up, it seemed some chilly little finger of winter air found its way down my neck. Watering eyes made it harder to navigate the wheelbarrow around the sheep. I never really got the hang of taking binder twine off a bale without removing my gloves.

A mild winter, in spite of higher temperatures, created its own trials. On the good side, during a mild and sunny winter there was usually a small stream running outside for the sheep to drink from.. There might be a bit of that fragile, crunchy ice—cat-ice, we call it—on the surface in the early morning, but the water is still gurgling along underneath, and the sun generally freed it before noon. That meant fewer trips with the water buckets. A three-gallon bucket of water weighs about twenty-five pounds, and the sheep needed eight per day; it was a relief not to have to make the requisite four trips with that load. On the bad side—the ground sometimes didn't freeze, which meant that twice a day I pushed a hay-laden wheelbarrow through a barnyard that the heavy fall rains had turned into sticky mud.

Sometimes I'd get both snow *and* mud. It was hard to keep up any kind of momentum with mud sucking at my boots and bury-ing the wheelbarrow wheel almost to the axle. The sheep loved it; my slower pace gave them lots of time to push around the barrow and snatch at the hay.

Never mind—winter is a peaceful time for the shepherd. And, by the way, few of us are out watching our flocks by night in De-cember. I'm pretty sure that the scholars who hold that Jesus was born in March have got the right of it. You only need to "watch", as in "be wakeful", during lambing. You can sleep at night for the rest of the year, and a good dog will warn you about predators.

Part of the Christmas story says that there was no room at the inn for Mary and Joseph, and so they were lodged in the sta-ble. Although "stable" generally implies horses and other riding beasts, the animals aren't specified. Tradition has filled that little stable with sheep and cattle, as well as the donkey. If you had to take shelter in a barn, a barnful of ruminants like sheep and cows really is the best choice. Ruminants create a lot of heat. An adult sheep puts out enough BTUs to qualify as a home-heating device. There's something peaceful about them, too, when they're lying around, chewing their cuds or just snoring (yes, sheep snore!).

Sheep can really take a lot of cold. Wool is a fantastic insulator, and gives off twenty-seven calories of heat per gram when it gets wet. Even a newborn lamb, once it is dry and has had a suck of milk, can tolerate twenty-below-zero temperatures as long as it's out of the wind. I lost several sheep one year during a brutal heat wave, but I've never lost an adult sheep to the cold.

As unscientific as this observation may be, I think one of the coziest sights in the world is a group of sheep in the snow. It makes me feel warm and rural and—oh, I'll admit it—Christmassy all over. There is a tradition that the animals in a barn all kneel at midnight on Christmas Eve, and sometimes even speak. In all the years I had sheep, I never checked on this one—there's enough harsh reality in farming that I preferred to keep whatever illusions I could.

Because the sheep stay close to the barn, and stay in a bunch, winter is a good time to work on taming the skittish ones. One winter I worked on getting my three young brown girls, Jynx, Kahlua and Kilim, to take grain from my hand. I had limited success, even though Kahlua was Folly's daughter, and Folly was one of my pet ewes. Since the sheep tend to form matrifocal mini-flocks within the larger group, ewe-lambs will usually follow their mothers' lead in behaviour towards the shepherd. If mom thought I was the Shepherd From Hell, daughter, and even grand-daughters, picked up on it. Elsie took years to tame down, and none of her line were pets except Honey, who was bottle-fed.

A friendly ewe, on the other hand, let her daughters know that I often had grain, or at least a scritch behind the ears, to offer an inquisitive sheep, and that made her line much easier to handle.

Winter was a quiet time to bond with my flock, to sit out in the barn and talk to them. Although we don't have a common language, in the winter I always felt as though they somehow understood what I said. I felt as though my sheep, my dog and I were all part of the same flock, despite the differences in species. With that feeling, who needed Christmas Eve and talking sheep?

Baling out

THE SECOND-LAST YEAR I KEPT SHEEP, the weather was so dry that there wasn't enough pasture for my flock. For the first time in nearly ten years I had to resort to feeding them hay through the summer. Even though I got a good deal on some hay from the previous year, it still made shepherding more expensive. It also made more work for me. Each morning I had to wheel them out four bales of hay, an activity which had its own hazards.

The common belief is that sheep are stupid. They aren't, really; they just don't think like we do. Mine were certainly smart enough to notice whenever I came out and got the wheelbarrow in the morning.

In other years, when the pasture was good, they were out at first light, nibbling away. That year they held back, waiting in the barn until the maid—me—arrived with breakfast. Actually, they didn't all wait in the barn. There was always a sentinel—one sheep, innocently standing around—"What, me? Watching for *you*? Naah, I'm just catching some sun."—who immediately gave out with "Here comes the hay!" Whereupon the entire flock barged out of the barn before the first two bales were halfway to the gate. They are a greedy lot, sheep. Every morning when I wheeled the hay out, I remembered that old shepherd's joke: You know why sheep have four hooves, don't you? It's to remind them of the four most important things in life—food, food, sex and food.

While they're greedy, sheep, with the exception of some rams, aren't malicious. This doesn't mean that there aren't hazards to dealing with them. When you're a shepherd, you have to remember your Bob Dylan—specifically, that line from "The Times, They Are A-Changin'" where he says "Don't stand in the doorway, don't block up the hall".

Sheep may not be as heavy as you are, but they aren't as tall as you are, either. Their centre of gravity is lower—translation, watch your balance, because they can knock you arse over tip with no trouble at all, especially when there are forty-five of them and one of you.

Another handy maxim is this: "Sheep don't care where your knees are". If they want to get through a doorway, and you're standing there, you'd better try to look threatening, or you're going to get sheep in the knees. Fortunately, a wave of the hand is often enough to make them balk long enough to give you a chance to get out of the way.

Now, perhaps you've spotted the flaw in this tactic—when I was wheeling a barrow full of hay, I didn't have a hand to wave at the sheep. I was too busy keeping the wheelbarrow upright and moving forward through the woolly mob. In some ways that was easier to do in the winter, in spite of the snow—or perhaps because of it. In the winter, I had a little groove worn between the gate and the place where I put the hay, and as the season wore on, the groove became deeper. It meant that, at worst, I was pushing on one sheep directly in front of me. In the summer, six or eight of

them could cram their heads into the hay around the front of the barrow, while the rest shoved for their turn or ran alongside me, hoping to catch a bite over the sides.

I really had to watch which sheep were crowding in right beside me. If it was Jet, or No-Name, or Specs, or even Laughing Boy, big galoot that he was, no problem. None of them had horns. But if it was Fudge, or Michaela, or Goblin or Gimlet, those curly, down-turning horns had a way of looping over my wrist or hand, and I had to keep alert to prevent having a wrist sprained.

Once the hay was down where they could get it, the sheep didn't find me that interesting anymore. Getting out of the barn-yard with an empty wheelbarrow was a whole lot easier than get-ting in with a full one.

Garm always came out with me and lay in the barnyard, watching the sheep while I fed them. It surprised me how many of our cats were also interested in the sheep, and vice-versa. One of our barn cats, Carmel, used to sit out with them in the barn-yard, and we'd look out and remark on our little orange sheep. Mog followed some of the lambs around, and also put up with the lambs following him, nosing at his tail. My female cats were much less eager, or more cautious. I did once take Lilith—also known as Dances With Dead Squirrels—into the barnyard, perched on a bale of hay in the wheelbarrow. She watched the sheep with interest until they began to swarm around the wheelbarrow, and then she was over my shoulder and out the gate. Did the sheep notice? No—what was so interesting about a tiny predator tearing for cover? Here comes the hay!

SHEEP ON THE ROAD

NANCY PEASE IS TO BLAME FOR ME being a shepherd. It was Nancy who introduced me to my favourite sheep, Icelandics. It was Nancy who invited us to spend weekends at her place during lambing season, so we could get our first experience with that wonderful time—and with middle-of-the-night barn checks. It was Nancy who included us in shearing day, showed us how to clip hooves and skirt fleeces, taking off the burrs and the bits of sheep manure, euphemistically called "dags". It was Nancy who sold me my first sheep, and my best ones.

When I felt confident enough in my abilities as a shepherd to start thinking about Icelandics, I went back to Nancy Pease for sheep. Nancy provided me with my two rams, Barley and Eystein, and she also sold me Michaela, my first Icelandic ewe.

Michaela was black, and a good breeder, although her fleece was really nothing to write home about. I drove our Caprice station wagon down to Shelburne at the end of May to pick her up. She was pregnant, and I wanted to get her home before her due date.

Of course, these things never work out as you plan them. The very morning I was to leave with Michaela, she went into labour.

The next day David and Nancy helped me load her into the back of the station wagon, along with her twin white lambs. Michaela had a thick bed of straw in the back of the car, and the lambs, one ewe, Freyja, and one ram, Fafnir, were safely bedded down in a box behind the driver's seat so that Mom wouldn't accidentally step on them or crush them.

"Get home as fast as you can," David advised me. "The biggest risk for the lambs is the heat."

"Shouldn't I stop to let them nurse?"

"They probably won't nurse," Nancy said. "The ewe can't stand in the back of the station wagon, and she won't likely let her milk down anyway."

With that in mind, I made as close to a beeline for home as the highways would allow. I made one bathroom stop at Nobel, at the Tim Horton's. I parked the car in the shade, rolled the windows down about two inches and dashed for the bathroom. Then I picked up a coffee and headed back out. I was lucky with lineups, and probably wasn't away from the car for more than ten minutes.

At Pointe au Baril, thirty minutes further north, I stopped to check on the lambs.

There was only one in the box.

Straw flew as I riffled through Michaela's bedding, thinking surely the lamb must have got out of the box and into the back with Mom. No lamb.

Now my knees were shaking. I looked at the rolled-down windows of the station wagon. No lamb in the box. No lamb in the back with Mom. I could only think that somehow, either while I was away from the car in Nobel, or—God help me—along the road to Pointe au Baril, the lamb had somehow squeezed out through the window.

It wasn't quite as unlikely as it sounds. Lambs are on their feet within minutes of birth, and are energetic and agile. They're also amazingly compressible and unbelievably brainless. And the evidence said that the lamb was not in the car, ergo...

I did the only thing I could think of to do. I started back along the highway towards Nobel, scanning the shoulders for a wet, white rag of erstwhile lamb. I saw nothing. I pulled into the parking lot at Nobel. No lamb. Obviously I would have to go into the Tim Horton's and ask loudly if anyone had seen a lamb in the parking lot in the last hour.

As I opened the door to get out, I heard a curiously muffled "Maa-a-a-a". It definitely hadn't come from the box. It sounded like it had come from the other side of the car altogether, and from lower down, as well.

I ran around to the passenger side, opened the back door and peered under the folded-down back seat. There, in the foot-well on the passenger side, scrunched between the seat and my overnight bag, was Fafnir, my missing lamb. Somehow he'd clambered out of the box, slid down between the door and the edge of the seat and crawled across the width of the car. I hauled him out and checked him over. He was unhurt, all limbs in place.

I tucked him back into the box and gave both lambs a little water from a baby bottle. Then I had to sit down for a minute and let my knees stop trembling. Finally I started the car again and drove home, an hour late from having to backtrack, but with all hands—or at least hooves—accounted for.

LAMBING AGAIN

THE END OF WINTER ALWAYS SEEMED to sneak up on us. One day we'd be cutting the annual balsam fir Christmas tree, and the next we'd have ravens in the barnyard, back from their winter migration and scrounging fleece for their nest. It was our signal to buy the annual bottle of selenium for the newborn lambs.

You need to give a newborn lamb a shot of selenium in Ontario, because there isn't enough in the soil to prevent white-muscle disease. The glaciers scraped it all down into Michigan eons ago. A lamb who doesn't get her shot will be, within a day or so, incapable of standing up.

As the lambs arrived, we could always tell who was Laughing Boy's get. Laughing Boy was a mutt sheep; his genes included Dorset and Suffolk and he was a big-boned, boxy animal. It was why we'd chosen him to be the terminal sire—farm talk for a ram whose progeny will be one and all heading for the table. His lambs were often—though not always—white, and had tight, short-curled coats. Romanov and Icelandic lambs, sired by Highway or Eystein, had a flattish, wavy or curly coat, and Romanov or Romanov-cross lambs are usually black. Besides, Romanovs and Icelandics are short sheep with slender legs, and Laughing Boy's lambs always looked like they'd been propped up on four logs.

The arrival of the first lamb always created a change in Garm's behaviour. All winter, if he were left unobserved for more than thirty seconds, he'd be in a head-down trot up the driveway and off to visit his girlfriend, Trixie, down in Wharncliffe. The upside was that we always knew where to go to get him. The downside was that we kept having to go to get him.

After the birth of the first lamb of the season, however, Garm abruptly abandoned Trixie. He spent his time curled up on the hay or in the snow, keeping an eye on his sheep. Once lambing started, we'd be in the barn trying to decide if the grunts and groans were labour or just sheep noises, while he lay in the dark just beyond the barn door.

The ewes didn't always appreciate his care and attention. A ewe with a new lamb stamps her feet at any perceived threat. Michaela, our lead ewe, was the friendliest sheep in the flock. When she was pregnant, she was a love-sponge. But this attitude didn't extend to Garm, who got a set of horns in the ribs if he came too close. Sheep horns curve backwards, so a butt usually doesn't involve points, but never mind. He yelped anyway, because Michaela gave it her all when she did connect. She was never particularly keen on Garm, or any of our other dogs, at the best of times, but at lambing she would actually chase them.

As the first due date approached, the ewes began to look like aircraft carriers—wide and round on the sides, flat on the top, They bagged up, their udders filling with milk. A day or so before she lambs, the ewe "drops"—that is, the lamb moves inside her and seems to sit lower. The visible sign of dropping is a triangular hollow right in front of the ewe's hip. Another sign is a ewe who begins standing around, or lying around, away from the main flock. When either of those things happened, I kept a closer eye on that ewe.

In years when we were lucky, and the ram was good, we'd probably have a whack of lambs all born about the same time, and then another lot about three weeks later. This is because a heat cycle is seventeen days, and younger ewes often don't get "settled" (that is, pregnant) on their first cycle. We'd have some from the first cycle, and then some from a later one, and a gap of a couple of weeks when you could sleep through the night.

In other years, whether it was that the rams were stargazing, or the normal variation in gestation simply didn't favour us, we'd go weeks without an unbroken night of sleep. We yawned all day, fell asleep in the afternoon and had energy for nothing but necessities. Garm wasn't the only one who gave up sex at lambing time—he was just the only one who did it voluntarily.

Even so, I still think fondly of lambing. Even if it played havoc with my sleep, my social life and my sex life, it was my favourite time of the shepherding year.

JOKER AND JYNX

I'M A SHEPHERD. MY SHEEP ARE SUPPOSED to regard me as her from whom all blessings flow—or at least as her from whom all grain flows. They are not supposed to see me as a predator. That's why it really upsets me when I have to act like a predator, and I am not referring to the annual roundup of lambs for the little tour of Northern Quality Meats. I'm talking about lambing.

Occasionally a ewe needs help lambing. Joker, a very small sheep, once needed my help to have a very large lamb. Two hooves and a nose poked out of her vulva and seemed disinclined to move any farther. They prairie-dogged in and out half a dozen times without any progress, and I could see that the lamb had its legs folded and tucked up under its chin. This made the shoulders wide enough to stick at the pelvic ring, the bone surrounding the birth canal. Until they straightened out, that lamb was going nowhere, no matter how hard Joker pushed. I'd have to straighten the legs, pulling gently on each hoof until the forelegs came forward and the shoulders narrowed enough to let the lamb slide out. But first, I had to get my hands on the ewe.

There are several ways to catch a sheep. The easy way uses sheep-handling equipment, fenced lanes which steer the sheep into small pens. We don't have this equipment.

The second way involves putting down a distraction, like hay or grain. Then, while the sheep stuff their faces, you can grab the hind leg of whatever sheep you need to catch, and *voilà*.

A ewe in labour is not easily distracted, not even, and this may be hard to believe, by grain.

And so we come to the third method. I talk softly and soothingly to the ewe and move slowly and gently closer to her until I am within grabbing range. Then I pounce. If you remove me from this picture and substitute, say, a cougar, you can understand my quandary. I want to help the ewe, but to get close enough to do it, I have to do things that set off all the little predator alarms in her head.

My sheep know me well enough that most of them will let me get hold of them fairly easily. Joker wasn't one of those. Still, I managed to snag her, press her against the barn wall with one of my knees planted behind her shoulder, and get hold of those hooves. Two gentle pulls straightened the legs, and the lamb's head began to slide forward.

I've never had a child, but my understanding of the process leads me to believe that few women are up to a thirty-yard panic sprint at any point after labour really starts. Please don't think this applies to sheep. The instant those legs straightened out, Joker was off like Donovan Bailey, out of the barn and gone. She quite literally peeled herself off her lamb and disappeared. I was left holding a slimy newborn lamb, umbilical cord and fat, pink placenta hanging down, and wondering where the hell Mom was.

I wiped the mucus away from the lamb's nose and mouth with a wisp of straw, then cut the umbilical cord and splashed

betadine on it. I checked the sex—female. Joker hadn't returned. I
left the lamb near the placenta, right where Joker had been standing just before she took off. I peeked around the barn door. Halfway up the field Joker stood braced and staring back down at the
barn. It seemed the best thing to do was whistle up the dog and
get out of her way.

That's what I did. As I closed the barnyard gate behind me,
I saw Joker take a few steps towards the barn, then begin to trot
back towards her lamb.

When I next went out to the barn, an hour later, she'd obviously done all the usual mothering things. I caught the lamb and
stuck my finger in her mouth. A lamb with a cold mouth hasn't
nursed yet, but the warmth of this lamb's tongue told me that
Joker's teats were open, and she was standing still for her baby to
nurse.

As far as I could tell, the lamb grew up normally, despite that
early experience of rejection. It could easily have been traumatiz-
ing for the lamb. I know it was pretty shocking to me. It's why I
like to have a tame ewe, because a tame ewe spares us all that kind
of early lambhood trauma.

I particularly wanted my brown ewes tame just to avoid that
very scenario—oh, all right, and because they were my favourites.
I spent a lot of time during the winter standing around in the
barnyard talking to them and handing out treats. The payoff came
when I went out to do a barn check and found Jynx, one of my
brown ewes, in labour. I sat down to wait with her. While it's best
to let the ewe take her own time, a ewe who isn't making progress
within half an hour of starting labour may need help.

Jynx resisted my efforts to tame her—she wouldn't take grain
from my hand, or even join the group of sheep pushing for the

opportunity. I was relieved that she let me get close to her and get hold of a horn without a predator-style grab.

In about twenty minutes she began pushing, a process which involves much neck-stretching and rolling of lips and eyes. After she had pushed hard half-a-dozen times, with nary a sign of a lamb emerging, I began to think I'd have to help.

She was amazingly quiet while I checked her rear and found two little hooves, tipped up so that the ends were caught at the top of the vulva, stopping the lamb's progress. A little tug on each hoof put things right, and in ten seconds there was a newborn lamb at my feet. Jynx lay down where she was and let me pull the lamb around to her head. She started to clean it up without paying any attention to me at all. This was the closest I had been to her since she was a baby. I didn't push my luck by trying to pet her—I didn't want to do anything to break this fragile calm, so uncharacteristic of Jynx around people.

Later she delivered a second lamb unaided, and was watchful but still calm while I gave her lambs their selenium shots, and checked that her teats were open. She even accepted a small handful of oats. But the next day, she wouldn't come to my hand, even for grain. She didn't bolt—she even put her nose within an inch of my fingers—but the truce was over. "I was tame when it counted," she seemed to say, "but I don't need your help anymore."

Well, companion animals they're not. Even if I still had to chase Jynx down for shots and shearing, I'll always remember the moments of rapport with this wary girl—all the more precious because they were rare.

EYSTEIN

NANCY PEASE, THE INSTIGATOR OF MY HAVING A FLOCK, tried to give us
some words of advice about the hard parts of shepherding. "Never
marry a ram"—she said, a bit of advice that sounds racier than it
is. It means that you should keep a ram two years as the "cleanup"
ram—the one who gets to breed the ewes the primary ram didn't
settle—and two years as the primary ram. Then you should get rid
of him, by trade or sale. She also once mused in a letter, "Never
fall in love with a sheep—or maybe never fall in love at all."

Farmers say "If you have livestock, you have dead stock." It's
a way of comforting ourselves when the inevitable happens and
animals—sometimes well-loved animals—die. It was no comfort
when my beautiful black Icelandic ram, Glen Osprey Farms Eystein, was killed by wolves in 1999 while doing the ram's job of
protecting the flock.

Eystein was a very gentle soul. Sure, he nailed a dog or two
during lambing season, and when it was time to square off with
the other rams for the ladies' favours he was as fierce in the lists
as any mediaeval knight. But of all the rams I've kept, he was the
one who never, ever offered to butt me, and who was always *fairly*

easy to catch. He would come over and put that big black nose in my hand even when I didn't have grain for him. I will admit that I could, and did on occasion, kiss him on the nose. Do not try this at home, kids. It's not recommended procedure. It's also pretty sentimental behaviour for a shepherd.

Rams are well-endowed. Once I had a group of ladies out to the farm, the wives of some Masonic types who were doing an afternoon's sightseeing while their husbands did secret male-bonding things. I got some grain and called the sheep. When the mobbing for hand-feeding got too rough, I poured the rest of the grain on the ground, whereupon the sheep turned their backs upon all assembled and began to guzzle. The ladies looked at all the south ends of these north-facing sheep. The ewes were nursing, and there were a lot of big, round udders. One woman pointed to Eystein's equipment and said, "I'll bet you get a lot of milk out of that one!"

"Well, not really," I answered, "but I *have* had a lot of lambs out of that bag."

Eystein fathered most of my brown ewes—brown is a hard colour to get because it is recessive to every other colour going in Icelandic sheep. But Eystein's father was a brown ram, so Eystein carried that gene inside his black hide, and I made sure that, however the ewes were divvied for breeding, his little harem included my brown and brown-carrying ewes. Jynx, Kahlua and Kilim were all his daughters, in addition to some of my black ewes. During lambing season, when we went out for middle-of-the-night barn checks, Eystein was usually found lying across the doorway of the barn, between his flock and whatever lurked outside. We could step over him without provoking so much as a snort, but the dogs walked wary of him.

A single wolf or coyote would have walked wary, too. It was a pack that killed him. A downed tree or broken branch probably reduced the kick of the electric fence, or pulled a section down low enough for the varmints to jump. I can imagine that they crept up on the sheep as they grazed through the bush.

The ewes took off immediately with their lambs, running for the barn, but rams don't react like that. Along with the harem comes the duty to protect it, and all Eystein's instincts would have made him turn on a predator without a thought.

Wolves and coyotes don't mess around; I'm sure they took him down as fast as they could. I hope that in his fighting rage he didn't feel much pain. I also hope that he left his mark on them, that there was a wolf or two who limped forever after. We never found anything of Eystein but some scattered fleece.

It may sound incongruous to say of an animal whose species is known for follow-the-leadership and lack of individuality that he had character and personality, but Eystein had both of those. The province paid compensation for him, because he was predator-killed inside the fencing. It was nowhere near enough to buy another ram of his quality. But even if it were, I'd never have found another ram of his character. For a sheep, he was pretty good.

WHEN THE STUDENT IS READY

ONE OF THE PLEASURES OF BEING A SHEPHERD is to wear a wool garment and to be able to tell people not only that I spun and knitted it myself, but also the name of the sheep who provided the fleece. I may not spin straw into gold but I can sure take hay, run it through a sheep to grow wool, and make yarn. Not so much straw into gold as hay into warm.

It's not exactly a dying art. There are thousands of women, and men, across North America who spin with wheels or spindles. Many have become shepherds to feed the habit.

Shepherding might have a genetic component, but I'm sure that there's also some kind of virus that causes it. Maybe you get it by touching a spindle, or sitting too close to someone already infected. Maybe it's carried on handspun, handknit garments. That last would explain how my friend Sienna got it. I was wearing a shawl made from the fleece of a grey-brown Romney-cross wether named Freak the last time we met.

Sienna and I attended the same women's retreat for several years. There were about sixty of us altogether, doing spiritual stuff and eating great vegetarian food, sleeping in cabins where six bunk beds and a shared bathroom transformed after-activities hours into a sort of pyjama party. We renewed, and made, connections ranging from lifelong friendship to email buddies, but I never expected to find, and certainly wasn't looking for, an apprentice.

It is said that when the student is ready, the teacher will appear. This sounds appallingly pretentious, but it seems to have worked that way for me and Sienna. A few months after the retreat I received an email from a woman from the event, passing on a query. Sienna was looking for me. She wanted to learn to spin. She was at teacher's college, and part of the curriculum was for the students to take three weeks and learn something new themselves. The theory was that they would, by consciously learning, understand the teaching process better.

I emailed her, suggesting some possible spinning teachers closer to Kingston, where she was studying. And that, I thought, was that.

The reply I got bubbled with enthusiasm. She didn't want just to learn to spin. She had a dream of sheep, and a rural life, and transforming wool into wonderful wearables.

"At first," she wrote, "I felt my little plan was totally unrealistic, and wasn't interested in getting it all in parts and pieces. I just naively hoped that there must have been someone else who dreamed this dream before me and ended up with a multitude of sheep and spinning wheels." She heard me confess on national radio to kissing my late lamented ram Eystein on the nose, connected the radio person with the woman from camp and decided I was just who she needed. Would I be willing to be her resource person if she could not, as she would love to do, plant herself among my sheep and wheels to learn from me?

How could I resist such enthusiasm? I love to spin, I love to get people turned on to spinning, and to sheep, and to the whole delight of making things. And I happened to have a guest room.

Further correspondence revealed that she had three weeks that fell—I couldn't believe my luck!—smack dab in lambing season. She said she'd be happy to share chores, make coffee, whatever she could do to help. Too good to be true, I thought—someone else to share shifts with. David would be home, too, but with three people to check on the beasties, nobody would go really short of sleep.

Yes, I did have a bit of ulterior motive, but at the same time, I was pleased and comforted to know that there are others who would at least like to have a crack at the life I chose.

"Come along, then," I said, and we fixed a day for her arrival.

Sienna arrived late in the afternoon, just in time for a minor farm emergency. Gimlet wasn't standing for one of her lambs, and while I hoped to get her to accept it in a day or two, I needed to keep it alive in the interim.

The first milk any mammal produces is called colostrum, and it's loaded with antibodies and other good things that disappear from the menu in a day or so. I needed to get some colostrum into Gimlet's lamb. Pat Ord, another area shepherd, had agreed to give me some frozen colostrum. When Sienna arrived, I was just leaving to pick it up.

"Come on along," I said, and she did. Sienna's first look at sheep wasn't my rather exotic Icelandics and Romanov-crosses, but the quintessential Canadian flock of miscellaneous white meat sheep.

In the eighteen days she stayed with us, Sienna went from a standing start of not being able either to spin or to knit to completing a shawl which she knitted from her own handspun yarn. She was also as good as her word about helping with the sheep. In fact, in addition to the lessons in spinning and knitting, she had a few other courses on her curriculum at Wharncliffe U.

Sheep Butt Assessment is the first course.("Is She In Labour Or Just Faking It?"). There's also Basic Ovine Obstetrics, in which she will learn how to sort out feet and noses, how a big lamb can squeeze through a small hole, and also that lambs come out covered in slime. As an adjunct to Sheep Butt Assessment, she'll learn Lamb Butt Assessment, or how to identify scours, and Veterinary Skills for Shepherds, or How to Give the Lamb the Needle Without Poking Yourself. There will also be a minor in Sleep Deprivation.

Sienna got along well with the sheep, and sat in on several births. More than sat in, really—when Michaela produced twins, both breech births, Sienna held onto Michaela like a trouper while I pulled the lambs out. They were covered with slime and blood, and so was I, and instead of retching or making "ooooh, yuck!" noises, Sienna's only comment was, "Elizabeth, you're a mess!" Pretty damn good for a city girl.

Sienna was a vegan, and didn't eat meat, dairy or eggs. She made us some good vegan meals while she was here, and she could also make a mean pot of coffee. Her sense of humour extended to naming one of the bottle lambs "Lamb Chop".

Sienna told me that one of her friends felt that my sheep were being exploited because I took their wool. Apparently some vegans object to people keeping animals for profit. That choking sound you hear is shepherds all over the country laughing hysterically at the concept of keeping sheep for profit. Seriously, I know many people do make money by keeping critters of various kinds, but it's not a problem with my flock—my sheep are net consumers, so I guess I'm okay.

One morning I looked out the bathroom window while I was brushing my teeth and saw Sienna unloading the morning hay from the wheelbarrow. Garm was beside her, waving his tail. The sheep mobbed around her in the usual way of sheep who see food in the offing, and she seemed quite comfortable with them. It was lovely to see—I'm always surprised how many people are cautious or fearful around sheep. She opened the bales, then wheeled the barrow away, passing out of sight behind the truck. When she didn't emerge on the other side, I knew what she was doing. She was getting the grain out of the back of the truck.

Unlike me, Sienna was a very slender person, and I had a sudden vision of my apprentice spinner mowed down and trampled into the ground by a thundering horde of grain-mad sheep. I tore upstairs to dress, gasping out to David what was happening. With what I regarded as totally unwarranted flippancy, he asked "Going to see if she's still vertical?"

She was. Not only was she vertical, but she was standing watching the sheep guzzle down their grain with that attitude of looking over the flock, seeing that everyone was there and behaving normally. Garm was leaning against her leg and looking up at her adoringly. Nobody needed picking up or dusting off. I doubt if the sheep cared that it wasn't me who fed them, as long as they were fed. Clearly Sienna was the Grain Goddess for that day!

When Sienna and I first decided on this idea of an apprenticeship in spinning, knitting and shepherding, I wondered if we would be able to stand each other's company for three weeks. After all, the old Viking maxim has it that fish and company stink in three days! But the time simply flew by. The day before Sienna had to leave, we blocked her shawl, stretching the damp knitting and pinning it into shape on the bed, pulling the lace pattern taut so it would dry smooth, open and beautiful. Several of the cats took it in turn to lie on the shawl to make sure it would block properly. Cats like to snooze on damp wool. The official reason is that wool actually gives off heat when it gets wet and the cats like the warmth. I also believe that there is some mystical connection between the number of cats who sleep on a garment pinned out for blocking and the success of the operation. I'm now convinced that no piece of knitting can be properly blocked without the use of at least one cat.

Sienna now lives in Toronto, where she works in outdoor education. I don't see her very often, but I think fondly of her. Her enthusiasm and persistence, and her delight in the sheep and everything we did together touched me deeply. I don't know if she'll ever realize her dream of keeping sheep, and I'm not sure whether she even knits any more. But she has a few good years left; I didn't even start keeping sheep until I was nearly forty.

Perhaps some day in the foggy future she'll sit in a barn somewhere, waiting for a ewe to get on wi't'job of pushing out a lamb, and it will cross her mind that she's sitting there in part because she chose spinning and knitting as her lesson in learning.

Sheep in the Blood

ALTHOUGH BOTH MY PARENTS CAME FROM FARMING FAMILIES, neither of them was interested in farming for a living. What I learned from them about farming could be summed up in five words: not all animals are pets.

When I began to think about keeping sheep, I learned from books. Later I learned from other shepherds. I certainly didn't learn about sheep from my parents. Before I knew any shepherds in Canada, the sum total of my experience with sheep consisted of a thorough reading of James Herriot and my first visit to Ireland in 1985 when I met Tex.

In the years I kept sheep, and particularly after I began to write about sheep, my father regularly said that he should get Richard and me together to talk sheep. I would really have enjoyed that, especially if we could have done it in Ireland. I haven't been there since my second trip in 1988, and though I did get my first hands-on experience with sheep on that visit, I was still a brand-new spinner and not yet thinking in terms of my own flock.

One of Uncle Richard's ewes had rejected her lamb, and he was feeding it. He didn't cuddle it in his arm and feed it from a baby bottle, as I'd always seen in pictures. Instead, twice a day my uncle found this little creature in whatever corner it had squeezed itself into, put a soft plastic tube down its throat and filled its stomach with milk. It took about ten seconds.

With the experience I've had since then, I can see that this lamb was determined not to live—it kept finding chilly, damp places to curl up in. At the time, in my naïveté, I suggested that it might do better if it were in front of the fire in the house, and not using so much of its energy to stay warm. My uncle would never have brought a lamb into the house. Toby, the dog, came in only rarely. But he humoured his niece and fixed up a basket for the lamb by the fire. The lamb died a day later. I suppose my memory is not so much of the lamb as of my uncle's kindness overriding the practicality of a man who lived by farming.

And now that I think of Uncle Richard and that lamb, I remember another thing—a day when my Aunt May, my cousin Jane and I were driving to Coleraine for groceries and lunch. It was a grey March morning, and a light rain was mizzling down over the green rolling fields and the hedgerows. March in Ireland is warmer on the thermometer than it is here, but the damp from the sea and the frequent rain meant that I was always chilly. I never went out without my wool jacket zipped and buttoned.

As we passed the fields, I saw Uncle Richard kneeling by a hedge. He was in work pants and shirt, hatless in the rain. His sleeves were rolled up past the elbow and his back bent—the top of his head was brushed by the ends of the branches in the hedge. It was such an unexpected sight that, even though we passed in a second or two, it is as clear to me today as it was that morning over twenty years ago.

"He'll be helping a ewe, there," said Aunt May, as we drove by. She thought no more about it. But I shivered in sympathy. What a contrast with James Herriot's sunny descriptions of his favourite time of year. I thought—James Herriot never seems to be kneeling under a hedge on wet ground. It's always a sunny spring day or a night in a cozy barn. In a flash I saw the difference between lambing for readers and lambing for farmers. We drove on into Coleraine, and I don't even remember asking my uncle in the evening about how that lambing went, whether it was a ewe lamb or a ram, single or twins, or how mother and baby were doing.

If I had been a practicing shepherd at the time, I would certainly have asked all those questions now—or, more likely, I would have asked Aunt May to stop the car so I could go and be there, see for myself what Uncle Richard did for the ewe and how he did it, learn something from a shepherd in my own family.

I'm sure Uncle Richard would regard me as pretty sentimental about the critters and the whole practice, but it's nice to think that shepherding is in the blood. It warms me to think that this business of keeping sheep didn't come totally out of the blue, but a little out of the red, too.

THE HYDRO SHEEP

I'M SURE YOU'VE NEVER HAD OCCASION to consider the imperatives of farm fencing. The dictum on fences is that they should be horse-high, bull-strong, and sheep-tight. Sheep tight. That's because sheep are the Houdinis of the barnyard world. Now, with the advent of electric fencing, perhaps some of that dictum can be modified. Cattle, with their big, flat feet and wet noses, get a good jolt out of even a conventional electric fence. I've seen horses grazing in a paddock enclosed by a single strand of electrified wire.

But sheep—well, there's a reason why the strongest electric fencing comes from New Zealand, where sheep outnumber people. With their tiny, hard hooves and insulating wool, sheep will pop through wires carrying a pulse charge of 8,000 volts unless those wires are tight enough to sing in the wind. It takes constant work, even so, to keep the flock within bounds. While I've herded sheep back into the pasture from as far as the Wharncliffe Cemetery, a mile down the valley, the incident that was the most trying was the one we call "The Hydro sheep".

The hamlet of Wharncliffe boasts not one, but two hydro-electric power dams—the Wells and the Rayner—right next to each other, although the Wells dam is a little lower. One August we got a call from a man at the Hydro installation.

"I think we have some of your sheep here," he said, "looks like a ewe and a lamb." I was surprised—the dam is over a mile away from our place as the crow flies, several times that as the sheep rambles. But when my husband David and I drove over, armed with a bucket of grain for bait, there were Horrible Nuisance and her lamb, disappearing down a wooded slope.

Horrible Nuisance had been a bottle lamb, and we'd named her because she was a particularly difficult lamb to ditch. She was fast and persistent, and clever about getting through the fence and following us back to the house. Although she eventually stopped following us—mostly because she was too big to slip through the fence easily—she'd kept the name. Now she was living up to it again.

The Hydro guy, Leo, told us there was a cliff at the bottom of the slope, and the sheep had nowhere to go. Leo didn't know sheep. I stayed on the upper slope, shaking the grain bucket gently to coax the sheep to me. Leo stayed on the road to head the sheep off, and David went slowly down to move them up the hill.

Well, they moved, all right, and Leo found that it is easier to head off a freight train than a sheep bent on freedom—freight trains don't deke like Rocket Richard. As for the coaxing properties of the grain, I might as well have been rattling a bucket of gravel. Horrible Nuisance and lamb disappeared at a gallop, this time up-slope towards the Rayner dam.

Did I mention that much of the Hydro property is nearly vertical, as well as wooded? We spent an hour crashing around in the bush before we got them penned into a narrow area where the only way to go was either down over a cliff or up-slope through the bush and under a guardrail onto the walkway of the Rayner dam.

This walkway was eight feet wide and made of concrete. On one side the buildings that housed the turbines kept them from falling down the face of the dam, and on the other a guardrail prevented workers from falling onto the steep wooded slope. The walkway was closed at each end by a locked gate.

Leo unlocked the gate and he and I lurked on the dam while David moved the sheep upslope. Sure enough, Horrible Nuisance and her lamb charged up onto the walkway, sliding under the guardrail like they'd been greased, and came straight towards us, David right behind.

Piece of cake, right? Wrong. While David clambered over the guardrail, Leo and I spread our arms to block as much of the walkway as possible. Horrible Nuisance was no fool—she dodged and jinked past Leo. I got a hand on her fleece, but only barely and she ripped out of my grip and charged for the gate Leo and I had come through. She bounced off it once, leapt at it again and flung it open—Leo hadn't closed the latch, and I hadn't checked it. Out she went, full tilt, back down the slope where we first saw her.

The lamb was only a few yards behind her and moving fast. I knew I didn't have a chance of getting hold of him. I could also see I wouldn't get to the gate in time.

Then David flew by me, like Superman without the cape, in a spectacular dive that brought him down right on the lamb. No matter how it bleated and kicked, he held on. In a few seconds it gave up the struggle and subsided to the occasional "blaaaaaaat!" Horrible Nuisance called once, but she definitely wasn't coming back.

Home we went with half our quarry, confident that we would have another go at the ewe. Sure enough, the following morning Leo called again.

"We spotted her!" he cried—I heard echoes of "View Halloo!" in his voice, and the belling of imaginary hounds. Leo wasn't the only one up for the chase—a second Hydro employee, Sam, had joined the ranks. Clearly this was better entertainment than electrical maintenance!

Once more up hill and down dale, after a wilier and now-alerted sheep. Twice we nearly had her, twice she eluded us. At last she jumped four feet down onto the top of the Wells dam. I dared to think we might finally catch her; the top of the dam was a narrow concrete walk that backed onto a wall, and butted the far end against the rocky, vertical side of the Mississagi gorge. Over the front of the dam it was a long drop to the river below, and on the near side David was already climbing down the ladder that led to the top of the dam.

"We've got her now!" crowed Sam, "She has nowhere to go!" I winced—when had I heard that one before? But perhaps this time it was true. Horrible Nuisance glanced around and, without a moment's hesitation, scrambled through the guardrail at the far end of the dam and onto a two-inch-wide ledge on the rocky face of the gorge. So much for "nowhere to go"! Now the big question was, did Horrible Nuisance know that sheep could swim? Would she plunge into the river rather than face captivity again?

Ten minutes on the ledge made up her mind for her. She tried to jump back through the guardrail, slipped, and skidded six feet further down the cliff-face until she found another tiny projection that held her. We couldn't reach her from the dam, and she clearly didn't want to swim. Would we have to leave her here and fetch her hay up daily? Would she become a tourist attraction, with postcards and radio interviews? Would she, in short, live up to her name even more thoroughly than she had to date?

Leo came to the rescue, appearing at the top of the gorge, some thirty feet above the dam, with a length of orange nylon rope. He made a slipknot and began lowering it gently. On the first try, he dropped the loop over Horrible Nuisance's head. I caught my breath as he lifted her—surely she'd hang or strangle? But he didn't jerk the line, and only a second later, David grabbed her out of the air. Two minutes later she was in the truck, up to her ears in the grain bucket and showing no ill effects from her ordeal.

After that, the worst I had to deal with for the summer was shooing a few sheep out of the wild roses and away from the water garden and putting them back in the pasture. It was hard to be really annoyed about it. We seemed finally to have got the fencing problems solved, however temporarily.

As for Horrible Nuisance, after her little adventure she seemed content to stay in the pasture. My only connection between Hydro and the sheep after that was the bill for running the electric fence.

BOTTLE LAMB

I INTENDED NEVER TO BE A MOTHER, but shepherds are sometimes co-opted into motherhood. I'm referring to bottle lambs.

Bottle lambs are those which have to be raised by someone other than their mothers, for any one of a variety of reasons. The ewe may die in lambing, or have too many lambs to feed, or the lamb may be out-competed by a more vigorous sibling. Sometimes the ewe will just plain reject a lamb.

This is what happened to the first lamb I bottle fed. Gremlin had twins, and although both her teats were open and I knew both lambs had nursed on the first day, by the second day she was not standing for the second lamb. Every time he tried to nurse, she would stamp and move away from him. If I didn't take a hand, he wasn't going to live. Fortunately, this lamb had already had colostrum. I could go straight to lamb milk replacer.

Any new baby needs small feedings at frequent intervals. To avoid going out to the barn at night more often than I have to, I brought the lamb into the house for the first couple of days and barricaded the little guy into the kitchen. I got used to doing my kitchen work with a lamb trotting around with me, his nose stuffed between my knees, where he thinks I ought to have an udder. When I was out of the kitchen, he wasn't happy—sheep need to be in a group, and he was lonely. A lonely lamb doesn't want to be able to see you from the kitchen, he wants you right there, preferably lying on the floor and snuggled up with him. I do have my limits.

Fortunately, I also had Garm, who took his sheep-dogging seriously. He would lie down and submit to having the lamb cuddle up against him. If he wasn't fast enough to lie down, the lamb was nosing about where Garm didn't have an udder, looking for lunch.

I had no doubts about the little guy's will to live—he sucked enthusiastically at the bottle. The danger is overfeeding—if you give them too much, they get diarrhoea. Unhealthy, nasty to clean off their backsides, and not something I wanted in the house. Although I couldn't feed him every time he cried, his constant bleating sometimes got to me, and I would sit with him and let him suck on my finger, which kept him happy and gave my ears a rest.

It was a relief to get the feedings down to the four-hour interval and move him back to the barnyard. It was also when I noticed that the maternal instincts that I do not have—or at least resist admitting to—kicked in, full force. I noticed it because I could unerringly pick out the voice of my lamb when he bleated. The first time this happened, I was really amazed—how did I know? Surely it was coincidence! But it happened every time. I always recognized his voice, and I can't, to this day, explain how.

The really hard part about a bottle lamb is weaning—weaning him from the bottle, and weaning him from me. He bonded to me, and wanted to follow me back to the house. Initially it was easy to shake him after feeding—I'd pop him in with the other sheep, or turn him to face away from me and then *run*. I could leave him behind easily—at first. Later it became harder; I'd some-times lurk at the top of the shop stairs, just outside the barn, for five or ten minutes until he gave up on me. I could have penned him in the barn and fed him there, but sheep are social animals, and it slways seemed cruel to me to pen a solitary lamb.

Why break the bond, why not keep the lamb as a pet? It's because my bottle lambs were mostly male, and a pet ram is a nuisance. They want attention; if they don't get it, they butt. It's a bump when they're little, but when they weigh a hundred pounds or more it's painful and can be dangerous. A pet ewe has a certain purpose—it's always handy to have one in the flock, because she'll come to the shepherd and the other sheep will follow her. But rams aren't flock leaders. So, yes, the lambs I spent extra care on almost inevitably were dinner.

This bottle lamb escaped that fate. Two days after we put him back out into the flock, we found him dead. He had worked him-self into a remote, wet, cold corner to sleep, far away from any other sheep, and died of hypothermia, or, more accurately, termi-nal stupidity. As farmers say, if you have livestock, you have dead stock. At least I had lamb milk replacer on hand for next year.

FIDDLE AND LAMB

WHEN YOU LIVE ON A FARM, you choose your cats for mousing ability rather than for their cuddlesome qualities. It's the reason I chose Fiddle, a skinny, green-eyed tortie with long paws and a fearsomely quick pounce.

Of course, I didn't know she was a good hunter when I got her. But her mother was a good mouser, according to my friend Nancy, whose grain storage was mouse-free, so it was worth the risk.

Fiddle was a cuddly kitten, round, with soft fur. As she matured, her baby fat melted away. She became a skinny, spooky, predatory cat, reverting to her cuddly kitten self only in pregnancy. When the kittens were weaned, she became Lurker-in-the-Shadows once again. My grain storage was mouse-free.

When Fiddle was five years old, I had a run of spontaneous abortion in my ewes. The distressing part was that the ewes miscarried late in the pregnancy. In the middle of the thrill and hustle of lambing, all that new life, my favourite part of the year, came the shock of lamb after lamb emerging from the womb, tiny, perfect and dead. Over half my lambs never drew breath, or had any possibility of it.

Belladonna was one of the last to lamb and, like most of the others, she delivered early. She'd shown no signs of imminent labour; no triangular hollow in front of the hip to indicate the lamb had dropped into position, no swollen udder, no nesting behaviour. She just pushed out a tiny black lamb, covered with the slime of birth, onto the manure of the barn floor and stood looking at it.

Without hope, I wiped the remains of the sac away from the muzzle and was astonished to hear a little gasp. The tiny thing shook its ears and produced a barely audible bleat. Belladonna strolled away. I tucked the baby, slime and all, into my jacket and headed for the house through the late-March snow.

I kept colostrum in the freezer for just this kind of emergency. While I was feeding the newly-dried lamb her first meal, Fiddle, who must have sneaked into the house on my heels, came creeping across the room and put a tentative paw onto my knee. Before she could pounce, I brushed her off.

"Not a mouse," I told her, although I could hardly blame her for thinking the lamb was prey. I could cup it in my hands with the legs dangling through my fingers. On my kitchen scale, it weighed a bare two pounds.

A newborn lamb must be fed every two hours. A barn full of lambing ewes has to be checked every three or four hours. I was already strained from the lack of uninterrupted sleep. Now I had a cat who'd decided that my bottle lamb was prey. Keeping Fiddle out of the house was impossible; she was not Lurker-in-the-Shadows for nothing. Time and again I found her at my knee as I fed the lamb.

I kept the lamb in a box with a towel and hot water bottle, in the spare room with the door closed. When I got up at night, I would check first to see if it was worth warming the bottle. I fully expected the lamb to die between one feeding and the next, but he hung on.

Finally the inevitable happened, and I failed to close the door properly when I went to get the bottle. Padding back upstairs in my nightgown, I was shocked to see a wide bar of light falling across the hall floor from the guest room.

When I got into the room, I could see that my worst fears were confirmed. Fiddle was in the box with the lamb. From the sharp motion of her head, she was biting. It was probably already too late. I didn't want to look. But I would have to put her out with her prey—I didn't want blood and guts on my guest room floor.

As I looked down into the box, Fiddle looked up. Her green eyes were slitted and she was purring. Her paws were wrapped around the lamb, who shook his wet, cat-licked ears at me and bleated. At the bleat, Fiddle turned and took the lamb gently by the neck, as I had seen her do with her kittens when they wouldn't hold still for washing. Then she went back to work on the lamb's face and ears.

I waited until she was done, marvelling, grateful and sleepily amused. When the lamb was washed to Fiddle's satisfaction, I gave him the bottle and tucked him back in. Fiddle curled around him, purring.

"Two points off your predator licence, Fiddle," I whispered, stroking her head. I went back to bed for another snatch of sleep. I left the guest room door open.

Roo, roo, roo your ewe

Spring arrives slowly in Northern Ontario, and in some places more slowly than others. I have, on occasion, found blue ice along one of our favourite canoe routes in May, and patches of snow in the bush in early June.

A cold winter never bothered me, or my sheep. An unseasonably warm one, however, created a problem for me—a problem peculiar to shepherds who keep primitive breeds of sheep, and particularly annoying to handspinners.

The sheep...shed.

The technical term for it is "rooing." It's the same physiological response that makes cats leave hair all over everything in the spring. The difference is that usually nobody is trying to collect cat hair to spin, and I wanted the wool from my sheep.

One warmer-than-seasonable late-winter day I watched Lilybelle, a black Icelandic-cross ewe, ambling across the barnyard. She was looking fluffier than usual, and I knew what that meant. It meant she was starting to roo, and that she'd be leaving pieces of soft, black, spinnable fleece all over Hell's half-acre, caught on trees and bushes and fence.

One of the reasons I kept Icelandic sheep was for the colour. There are lots of sheep who have lovely fleece, but most of them in Canada fall into the big-hornless-white-woolly category. Most of *those* are destined for the table. For most shepherds, shearing is something you do because the slaughterhouses penalize you for shipping an unshorn sheep, and wool is a byproduct, or even a liability. For me, wool was the main reason for my sheep.

The sheep that roo are older breeds, called "primitive". Shetlands and Icelandics are primitive breeds. The fleece actually breaks naturally, close to the skin, and the fibres come loose and can be easily pulled away. It has a couple of advantages over shearing. For one, there's no risk of "second cuts"—short bits created when the shearer runs the shears twice over the same part of the sheep—and of course no risk of cutting the sheep or giving it razor burn.

It also has disadvantages, and I was looking at one of them as a flap of wool fell down Lilybelle's side and trailed along the ground. If I didn't get out there now and get that wool, I was going to lose it. I'd have to catch Lilybelle to peel it off, and while I was at it, I'd check for any more loose wool. It was a sure bet, though, that not all of it would be loose, and I'd have to do this several times.

I also knew that, after dangling a week of springlike weather in front of us like a string before a kitten, winter would thump us with two feet of snow in three days and crank the temperature down to minus twenty-five Canadian. As sure as shooting, if I rooed out that lovely fleece, Lilybelle would have to face that weather without her built-in winter woollies.

I was tempted, for a moment, to let it go a little longer. Just then the competition showed up. A raven swooped in and landed on a fence post. It cocked its head, and I could almost see the thought-bubble forming above it—"Oooooh, look! Nesting material! Pretty!"

I know ravens are clever birds, and I'm sure they deliberately go after the fleeces I particularly want myself. There were at least two white sheep rooing as well, but the raven fluttered to the ground, pecked once or twice and then casually hopped towards Lilybelle.

That settled it. I found a milk crate and a feed sack and started towards the barnyard. As I approached the gate, the raven took off again, circled around in a tight little arc and landed gently on Lilybelle's back. She never looked up. Delicately, the raven dipped its head.

"Hey!" I yelled.

The raven looked sideways at me and took off, trailing a beakful of soft black fleece.

Between us the raven and I managed to spook Lilybelle. She stared at me, feet braced as though to bolt. I set down the milk crate and the feed sack and went to get a handful of grain.

A few minutes later I had her up on her rump. While the raven watched from the top of a nearby balsam, I gave Lilybelle the first installment of her spring haircut.

SHEARING DAY

SHEARING DAY USUALLY DESCENDED upon us like the wolf on the fold. One year we thought we'd have to call our shearer and put it off, because the heavens had poured, and the sheep were wet. But the next day was sunny and windy, perfect sheep-drying weather, and all was set to go when Jim called to say that he would be out the following morning at eight.

Jim Olding, the shearer, was a New Zealander transplanted to Canada. His day job was with one of the many companies in the forestry industry here in Northern Ontario, but he spent a lot of time in the late spring and early summer shearing for local sheep farmers. He learned to shear in New Zealand, where it's an honourable trade and the money for it is good. When he moved to Massey he saw the need for a shearer here, and stepped into the breach.

I never tired of watching sheep shearing. Even now, years after I've last seen it, I'd still be happy to watch a shearing day. Aside from the rhythm of it and the marvel of a whole fleece coming off in one piece, there is the amazing and amusing transformation of a bulky, woolly sheep into something more like a dairy goat with a buzz cut. Even their little tails were shorn. Jim used to leave a

humourous little poodle-tuft on the end of the longer tails. Afterwards, it took me a few days to get used to the sleek, shorn shapes
of the adult sheep. The lambs, still in their woolly coats, looked
twice as fluffy and adorable by comparison.

I once read that shearing a sheep was "more like dancing than
fighting". Jim knew the dance—you could see it in the way he
tipped a sheep onto her rump in ten seconds, and moved her
around so he could reach to shear every part. Even a panicky
young ewe was under control and amazingly calm. As for Laughing Boy, our Dorset-cross ram, that pony-sized critter was putty in
Jim's hands, gazing meditatively at the barn ceiling as his fleece
peeled off in one great blanket under the shears.

It's the shearer who keeps the sheep calm—Jim told us that
the first rule of shearing is: Never, never lose your temper. If the
shearer is angry, the sheep are tense and uncooperative. You waste
time and energy turning that dance into a fight. The second rule?
Don't cut off the teats. Half a day with Jim saw our little flock
beautifully shorn, and at what seemed to be a fairly relaxed pace
for him. If we were to do it, we'd spend three days at it.

I also loved, still love, the smell of the freshly-shorn fleece.
Especially on a warm day, the smell of the lanolin and wool is
strong, comforting and homey. A ram fleece has a sweet, almost
berry-like smell. I always took the job of removing the fleeces after
each sheep was shorn and skirting them to remove dirt, manure
and any fleece too tangled with hay and chaff. The lanolin made
my hands feel soft and smooth, and the smell of the sheep was
all over my clothes, just from bundling up and bagging the fresh
fleeces. Shearing was a happy time, the next best thing to lambing. Those fleeces were pregnant with possibility—wool to sell, or
to spin, or to send out to be spun.

At one time I dreamed of making a yurt, one of those circular felt houses the Mongol sheepherders live in as they graze their flocks. I sometimes thought it would have been lovely to live out in one, herding my sheep across the beaver meadows and bush of Algoma, a peripatetic shepherdess of the new world north.

Of course it wasn't practical. For one thing, a bear would walk through a wall of wool as though it weren't there. I settled for keeping that a lovely fantasy, and instead made shawls, gloves and hats from my own fleeces, remembering with each one, the sheep it came from.

The cursed sweater

My friend Nancy Pease is a prolific and generous knitter. As the year 2000 approached, she wasn't thinking so much of Y2K, except to name the new housecat Y2Kitty. Actually, I believe that name was her husband David's idea. What *she* was thinking about was knitting runic sweaters to celebrate the millennium of the Viking arrival in North America. We don't really know when the Vikings actually arrived, but what the hey, the year 2000 is as good a millennial anniversary as you're going to get.

I like runes, the angular script used by various northern peoples to inscribe stones, swords, whatever might need a handy "Leif made me" or "Sigrid was here". Our set of letters is called the "alphabet", from the first two letters, alpha and beta. The runes are called the "futhark", because the first letters spell—well, "futhark".

There are several versions of the runes, depending on when and where they were used. The Anglo-Saxons had a slightly different futhark from the Norse, and the Germanic futhark is different again. During the era when the runes were in use they were mystical as well as practical. In a largely non-literate society, the concept of making speech, which was audible but invisible, into writing, which is visible but inaudible, was mysterious and dangerous. Runic inscriptions were used for magical workings, and still are so used by some who believe in magic.

The story of how the runes came into the world is one of the central Norse myths. Odin, the chief god of the Norse, hung for nine days and nine nights on Yggdrasil, the ash-tree that holds up the worlds. At the end of that time he gouged out one of his own eyes, and the runes appeared before him in the air. He seized them before he lost consciousness, and brought the knowledge of writing into the world. With origins like that, it's little wonder runes are considered magical.

The runes are admirably suited to knitting. They're made of horizontal, vertical and forty-five-degree angled lines, all easy to graph as a knitting pattern. Several times Nancy had asked me to come up with runic inscriptions for sweaters for specific people.

The first time she actually requested a spell. A friend of hers had been diagnosed with breast cancer and had opted for the radiation, *sans* surgery. I got out my dictionary of Anglo-Saxon English and my runes and came up with something that I thought would do the trick. I graphed the runes for knitting and Nancy made the sweater. While I'm not prepared to take credit for the outcome, the truth is that the cancer receded after the treatment.

"Have you ever thought of runes for a sweater for yourself?" Nancy eventually asked me.

"Not really," I replied.

"Well, start thinking," Nancy said, "because I'm making a sweater for you, and one for David."

David came up with his own inscription immediately.

"I want 'I like plants that bite back,'" he said. David raises carnivorous plants.

I put the sentence into runes. My own inscription gave me more trouble. I like the Hávamál, the Words of the High One, which is a compilation of Viking sayings. "Judge no day until evening" is one. "Judge no maid 'til she's bedded, no wife 'til she's buried" is another. There wasn't one about sheep, so I graphed "Judge no sheep until shorn" and then, on impulse, "If you have livestock, you have dead stock". I can't think why I did this, except that it was late, and I was tired and feeling a little punchy.

Nancy responded to David's choice with, "Don't come running to me if you get poison ivy." She said nothing about mine until the sweater arrived in the mail. It was a beautiful cardigan, thick and warm, knitted in dark brown handspun with a runic inscription in white around the yoke. With it was a letter. The contents of the letter were so surprising that I can quote them almost verbatim, years later.

"What possessed you," she wrote, "to put 'If you have livestock' into runes? And what possessed me to choose it? Saturday I started your sweater. Saturday night we camped out on the property. I managed to get the first pattern row set and do one more row before the light failed.

"About two in the morning we heard the sheep fussing. Himself [her husband, David] got up, but it was too dark to see anything.

"In the morning, two of the black ewes were dead. Nadine [one of their dogs] ran down to us and grovelled at my feet like I was Pharaoh's wife."

The injuries on the ewes showed that they'd been killed by a dog. Dogs grab and worry at the flanks and hindquarters of a sheep, and they kill almost by accident. A wolf or coyote would have hamstrung the sheep, taken out her throat and killed her efficiently.

Unfortunately, once a dog has attacked sheep, and particularly killed one, no sensible shepherd would keep her. Breaking a dog of sheep-killing is almost impossible. Nadine had to go.

"David shot her," Nancy's letter continued, "and buried her with the ewes by the gravel pit.

"When I went back to my knitting I realized I'd brought it on myself, and there was no point taking the pattern out now. Wear it in good health."

I smiled at Nancy's rather uncharacteristic attribution of Nadine's killing spree to the runic inscription. She was usually very down-to-earth.

Strange enough, but it got stranger. After the sweater arrived, my sheep began to die of "pulpy kidney" (enterotoxaemia), a problem I had never had before. Enterotoxaemia is caused by a too-sudden increase in nutrition. I hadn't changed anything about my flock's feed, and I was mystified as to the cause. Nothing I did seemed to stop the deaths.

In a moment of desperation, I performed an exorcism on the sweater. I couldn't think of anything else to do.

Here's the spooky part. Once I did that, no more sheep became ill, and all but one of the ones that were doing poorly recovered.

I can't explain it, and I don't intend to try. But I do know this—I'm very, very careful now of what I put into runes.

THE BOYS

Biology being what it is, if you have sheep and you want lambs, you will need at least one ram. In the happy, fluffy world of shepherding, the ram is often the catch.

An aggressive ram is a good ram—high testosterone levels make a ram what is called an "eager breeder", and also make him hard to handle. Nancy once had a ram whose aggression level was so high that you *couldn't* dominate him. Ivar the Wicked Ram, they called him, and eventually they called him "sausage".

Neil Meatherall was once knocked down by a ram that butted him full on the side of the leg, and was so badly bruised he didn't get out of bed for two days. Neil is not a little man, and the ram was not a large one. Another ram refused to accept his place in the pecking order—or should I say, head-butting order?— and got himself killed by the other rams in a single morning. High on belligerence, low on brains; clearly an animal it's hard to reason with.

Apparently the only way to keep a ram in line is to make sure he knows you're bigger than he is.

"Well, of course you're bigger than he is!" I hear you cry.

No, you're taller. It's not the same thing. In fact, it's a definite disadvantage. If you weigh, like me, something over one hundred and fifty pounds, and something that weighs eighty pounds hits you in the knees, three feet of extra height is no help—besides, you won't have it long. You'll be on the ground.

So how *do* you convince a ram you're a bigger ram? With a hammer, they tell me, and I believe it. You can see why, the more I thought about keeping sheep, the more I read about them, and the more friends' experiences I heard, the more my thoughts revolved around the ram.

I've never had a ram who was as belligerent as Ivar, nor as stupid as the butted-to-death ram. Considering some of the horror stories, I've had good luck with my boys, and have regarded them all fondly.

Laughing Boy was our "terminal sire"—meaning his offspring would all go to Northern Quality Meats. He was a huge ram, like a pony with wool, and a docile and mild-tempered animal. Laughing Boy was built as a good meat sheep should be. He had a large, rectangular body with a leg at each corner and a head at one end. What he didn't have was horns, and he was, in consequence, very hard to catch. Once you had hold of him, he didn't struggle, but getting hold of him usually involved a flying tackle to get your arms around his neck. Our other rams all came equipped with easy-grab handles; stretch out an arm at a strategic moment and you could snag a horn without too much difficulty. His docility never seemed to interfere with his ability to breed.

Barley, my brown Icelandic ram, was Laughing Boy's temperamental opposite. He was high on the testosterone, higher than any other ram I ever owned. I know this because once I disobeyed a cardinal rule of sheep-keeping, which is, "Never turn your back on a ram in breeding season". I suppose I was complacent, because most of my rams have been relatively gentle—although Eystein was the only one I'd kiss on the nose—and I got careless.

I went out to the barn in the evening, for whatever reason, and as I picked up a loose piece of binder twine, I suddenly saw stars. It was after that burst of light and colour and "What the hell?!" that the pain hit; a sharp, hard pain in my head as my stunned brain finally caught up with the impact of my skull on the barn wall, and another hard pain in my butt. That, of course, was Barley's head on my well-padded posterior.

I straightened up, still dizzy, and laid my hands on the first thing available, which was a section of lambing pen. David made the pens in four-foot-square panels—four two-by-fours bolted together, with a fifth one across the middle. They were solid suckers, and I picked this one up and swung it through a hundred-and-eighty-degree arc to connect with Barley's skull as he moved in for another hit. He backed off, shaking his head, and I took my opportunity to escape.

As I stumbled back to the house through the dark, I realized that I was no longer wearing my glasses. I remember the sky as being incredibly clear, dark and starry, although some of those stars may have been in my head.

"What happened? Are you okay?" David asked, as I stepped into the kitchen and fell against the door frame.

"Barley hit me," I said, "and my glasses are somewhere on the barn floor. I couldn't see to find them."

David guided me to the couch and I sat there with my eyes closed while he retrieved my glasses—both pieces—and made me a cup of tea. After a good night's sleep I felt better, except for a scalp bruised in two places.

I wasn't angry at Barley, or afraid of him, either, but I certainly never turned my back on him again, at least during breeding season. Eventually Barley was killed by coyotes or wolves. As far as we can tell, the flock ran away, and he didn't. He was doing the ram's job, fighting off predators. All we found of him afterwards was a stomach full of chewed grass and a scattering of brown wool.

Fafnir, the lamb who'd disappeared from my car between Nobel and Pointe au Baril as a newborn, grew into a big bruiser of a ram, too. He wasn't as aggressive as Barley, but he was certainly a force to be reckoned with.

After Barley was killed by coyotes, Eystein stepped into the top-ram spot. As soon as the sheep were out on grass again, he drove Fafnir and Laughing Boy away from the ewes, so forcefully that they broke through the fence and lived wild in the bush for most of the summer.

We saw them from time to time—two big, white animals cruising the edges of the field—but they became wary, and certainly didn't want to come back inside, where Eystein was waiting to make it clear how welcome they weren't. They were a bachelor flock of two, livin' the free life, hangin' out in the wild places.

In the fall David took a bucket of grain and managed to coax them back into the field. When he had them safely inside again, he told me where he'd found them.

"They were down in the beaver meadow," he said. The beaver meadow is a large, flat area of lush grass. It had once been the bottom of a beaver pond, until the dam broke and the water rushed away downstream, leaving the erstwhile pond high and dry. The grass throve in the rich pond-bottom soil, and Fafnir and Laughing Boy throve on the grass.

For water, they had the creek that ran through the middle of the beaver meadow, and for company, a young bear who left his traces all over the meadow on the far side of the creek. The bear never crossed onto the boys' side. David figures that he looked at the two big, white critters and thought, "What the hell are those? Not going near them!" It probably helped that Fafnir's horns had grown into a curve that left the points sticking straight forward.

We also had Highway, a Romanov ram who came home with me as a lamb along the Trans-Canada one spring. I'd learned my lesson with Fafnir; I gave Highway no chance to make or fake an escape. He travelled on the passenger-side floor of the front seat; my niece lent me her laundry bag, and I tucked Highway into it with the cords snugged around the base of his neck. He tried once or twice to stand up, but couldn't extend his legs. Instead he lay quietly the whole way, peeing at intervals, but otherwise no bother at all. He seemed quite calm, too, chewing his cud and snoozing. I'd finally figured out the lowest-stress way to transport a lamb.

My niece didn't want the laundry bag back. It was too bad I had no more use for it; Highway was the last sheep I ever bought.

Envoi

SOMETIMES IT'S HARD TO BELIEVE that my shepherding days are over. A
few years after we got Highway, our enthusiasm for fencing through
the bush and chasing sheep back into the field waned. Then David
bought a pet store, and the sheep were redistributed, some to other
shepherds, and some to freezers. It's been seven years or more since
I had a sheep, and while I might still be able to sling a bale or dodge
a ram, it would be much harder work than before.

Every now and again I come across some reminder—a skein
of yarn, a photograph. When David and I were finally legally married, I wore my Honey shawl, and thought fondly again of that
ewe and of several other pet sheep.

A whiff of fresh fleece catapults me back to shearing days,
and I still feel nostalgic for the particular smell of a barn at lambing, that scent compounded of sheep, hay and fresh, raw placenta.
I remember how startled I was the first time I recognized the voice
of a lamb I bottle-fed, and I remember the feel of Eystein's nose,
warm and soft and a little bristly with whiskers, in my palm.

At its best, keeping sheep is—more of the same. You feed your
sheep, do the shearing and the vaccinations and the hoof trim-

ming, the breeding and the lambing, without incident, without catastrophe, the same this year as last and stretching on into the foreseeable future.

Maybe this sounds boring to some people. Some crave excitement, adventure, really wild things, the fast lane of life. Some prefer a back road where the big surprises are a stand of fiddleheads in the spring or a sandhill crane calling from the neighbour's field.

I miss the sheep talk, too. Have you ever had one of those telephone conversations that start "Well, there's really nothing new happening here..." and then you go on to talk for an hour? When shepherds get together, they do what any other group does—they talk shop, or, in our case, sheep. Some years ago David and I went to Fiberfest in Kalamazoo, Michigan. On the first night we sat around a campfire with a group of other vendors—spinners, weavers, felters, woodworkers, sheep people all. We had a sociable beer or three, and for hours we talked about sheep. We talked about the different breeds we, or our neighbours, or someone we knew, kept. There are so many breeds of sheep, breeds with wonderful names. Border Leicester and Blueface Leicester, Scottish Blackface, Rough Fell and Romney Marsh, Finn, Icelandic and Gotland sheep, all named for their place of origin, like the Suffolk, the black-faced white animal that is the common image of sheep. The names could be a soothing murmur to the sound of the wheel, or a jump-rope chant.

Corriedale, Cotswold, Coopworth, Karakul;
Jacobs, Shetland, Lincoln Longwool!

And we swapped predator stories. Whether you say COY-oat, KY-oat or ky-O-tee, every shepherd has a story about the varmints.

Bears, wolves, coyotes and dogs, who preys on your flock? What's the best protection—sheepdog, llama, donkey? New Zealand electric fence, or the old North American standard, and remember the time you tried to step over it...?

We talked colour and fleece, shearing, breeding and lambing, belligerent rams and bottle lambs. The next day we talked all day to our customers and the vendors around us about spinning, weaving, sheep, angora rabbits, goats, llamas...and that night, around another campfire and a few more beers, we got together and did it again—three or four or five more hours of stories and opinions and experiences from the sheepfold.

Shepherding, and perhaps any profession, is like a secret society, with its own passwords and mysteries. "Staple" to a shepherd is the length of the fleece, not a metal U for holding papers together. Dag, skirt, cleat, crutch, all have strange and mystical meanings, known only to sheep people.

We even had our own jokes. At the time Jack Kemp was running for office in the States, and one of the shepherds grumbled, "I thought the point was to get the kemp out!" We all laughed uproariously, but it was only funny if you were a shepherd and knew that "kemp" is unwanted coarse hairy fibre in the fleece.

Although it's been so long, I still have a soft place in my heart for sheep, and for those who keep them. I still have stories, and fond memories, and sometimes I wonder if my shepherding days are truly done. With sheep, or, I suppose, with any passion, the problem is not where to start. It's always where to stop. Even without the actual sheep around any more, the stories remain. I hope you've enjoyed them.

Author Note

ELIZABETH CREITH'S PUBLISHING credits include fiction, non-fiction, memoir and poetry, and a decade as a freelance writer/broadcaster for CBC Radio. She is probably best remembered for her time as Shepherd in Residence, and for her children's book *Erik the Viking Sheep* (Scholastic Canada, 1997). She believes that art is an essential part of life, and that too much housework rots the soul.

Elizabeth studied fine art and mediaeval language, literature and history, hardly proper preparation for raising sheep in the bush in Northern Ontario. She draws heavily on her knowledge of myth, history, folklore and animals in her writing. Her fiction, humour and poetry have been published in print and on line since 1990, and she is currently working on a young-adult fantasy novel. Elizabeth lives and writes in Wharncliffe, Northern Ontario, distracted occasionally by her husband, dog and cat. She blogs about writing, art and life at http://ecreith.com